SUPERFOOD JUICES

100 DELICIOUS, ENERGIZING &
NUTRIENT-DENSE RECIPES

SUPERFOOD JUICES

JULIE MORRIS

author of *Superfood Kitchen*

STERLING
New York

STERLING
New York

An Imprint of Sterling Publishing
387 Park Avenue South
New York, NY 10016

© 2014 by Julie Morris
Photography © 2014 by Julie Morris
Photos on cover and pages i, vii, 1, 6, 11, 18, 29, 33, 36, 39, 42, 51, 55,
59, 61, 68, 70, 80, 94, 100, 102, 105, 110, 120, 138, 141, 143, 144, 146,
149, 172, 191, 193, 197, and 214 courtesy of Oliver Barth

ISBN 978-1-4549-1077-0

Distributed in Canada by Sterling Publishing
c/o Canadian Manda Group, 165 Dufferin Street
Toronto, Ontario, Canada M6K 3H6
Distributed in the United Kingdom by GMC Distribution Services
Castle Place, 166 High Street, Lewes, East Sussex, England BN7 1XU
Distributed in Australia by Capricorn Link (Australia) Pty. Ltd.
P.O. Box 704, Windsor, NSW 2756, Australia

For information about custom editions, special sales, and premium and corporate purchases,
please contact Sterling Special Sales at 800-805-5489 or specialsales@sterlingpublishing.com.

Manufactured in China

2 4 6 8 10 9 7 5 3 1

www.sterlingpublishing.com

CONTENTS

INTRODUCTION

"ASTONISHING PERSONAL TRANSFORM-ATION!" followed by a train of additional exclamation points, stock-art graphics, and Photoshopped bikini photos is not something I can blast across my personal "juice" story. I must confess, my launch into the world of rejuvenating juices isn't the sort of dramatic tale of which advertising dreams are made. No, initially, we were simply having a party . . .

Let me tell you a little something about the fleeting weeks that comprise "summer" in Portland, Oregon: They are sheer Peter Pan magic. There is a glow about the whole city, as if the sun has nothing better to do than shine down on the wonderful city and bring happiness . . . a dramatic contrast to the drippy gray ceiling that lurks over the skyline for the rest of the year. The Portland summer city scene is like a page out of a musical: There is ubiquitous bike riding; waving neighbors; waving strangers; random street art (now you know where all my embarrassing college paintings are circulating); artisan coffee shops, each better than the next; grassy parks; picnics in grassy parks; make-out sessions in grassy parks; a flood of terribly great music; a flood of greatly terrible music; local edibles that range from authentic Thai to homey vegan to James Beard Award–winning cuisine; flowers *everywhere*; and a city-wide play-ground spirit that promotes the mantra "there's always fun to be had." To this day, I wish I had a camera handy the time I was walking down a busy street and saw a man, who was dressed up as Batman for some reason, pass another man, *also* dressed up as Batman, and then witness the "Batmen" exchanging a high-five before carrying on with whatever it is you do when you're casually dressed up as Batman. If anyone asks you "why?" in Portland, a simple "because" is a more than ac-ceptable answer. And for a couple of years, I had a very important part to play within this eclectic tapestry: I was "the Juice Girl."

At the time, I was working with a local, family-owned organic juice company that made the best fresh-pressed juice around (they had a farm an hour outside of the city in Hood River, where they grew much of their produce)—an occupation that, admittedly, caused my occasional juice habit to evolve into one of staggering proportions. Like so many things in Portland, my job requirements were rather random, and one of my responsi-bilities was to go to different health food stores, co-ops, events, and festivals, and get people to try our juice. This was definitely the kind of job that fell more on the side of simple awesomeness, and less on the side of actual skills, since there were really only three basic requirements:

1. Stand around.
2. Talk to people.
3. Drink juice.

Due to the sheer number of people I talked to about juice each week, and because I often frequented the same health-conscious spots in the city, developing some form of "juicy" reputation around me was practically inevitable. But what amused me more than anything else about this local "fame" was that it was not solely limited to regular health food store habitués; it stretched into the Portland community. "Oh hey, you're the Juice Girl," the heavily tattooed guy locking up his bike next to me on the street would say, surprised. Indeed, I was the Juice Girl.

The second summer I spent in Portland, my neighbors and I decided to have a block party. You know, just a close down the street in the middle of the city and fill it with music,

alcohol, and as many people as possible type of party (because apparently you can just go ahead and do that in Portland). I was tasked with the all-important job of, you guessed it, supplying juice—clearly a job I could handle. The juice warehouse where I worked was equipped with a walk-in refrigerator that was easily four times the size of my apartment at the time, and was basically juice heaven: boxes upon boxes of juice of every possible variety, color, and flavor, each more delicious than the next, stacked and ready to be distributed throughout the city. Because it was all fresh-pressed and only flash-pasteurized, the juice had a particularly short shelf life, meaning there was always excess juice to be either donated to charity . . . or enjoyed by thirsty employees. I brought this juicy excess—grapefruit, red ginger limeade, carrot, mango, you name it—to our street party, as if it was *my job* to distribute it to the people and hydrate everyone in the city.

Our party grew the way any great party does: diligently spider-webbing from friend to friend, to friends of friends, to friends of friends' casual acquaintances, to people who really had no business being there at all (but of course were welcome), and even to the random fire dancer who showed up to perform a little after midnight. And while my neighbor was still pouting that we weren't able to fill the entire street with sand, as he had so earnestly hoped, my juice donation was a huge hit. Though we had extra food and even extra alcohol after the evening had ended,

I'm proud to say that the juice was *gone*. There was literally not a single drop left over. But, then again, I wasn't really surprised. Through my work as the Juice Girl, one thing had been made abundantly clear to me: *Everyone. Loves. Juice.*

As babies, we consume mother's milk as the perfect source of high-density nutrition, getting the minerals, vitamins, protein, and sugars we need to grow. In many ways, juice is like an adult version of this milk. It's easy to consume, easy to digest, and hyper-packed with nutrients. In fact, consuming the equivalent of an entire fruit bowl or basket of vegetables can be just a few convenient, delicious sips away. Drinking juice offers an instinctual pleasure and a natural high. The act feels good, tastes good, and makes you yearn for more. Our bodies soak up this pleasurable, profoundly visceral experience like a sponge, and we feel energized afterwards.

A week after our street party, I was "working" (see aforementioned skill set) at an outdoor event promoting juice, and a young woman approached me. "I *loooove* these juices," she cooed, drinking a sample. "I like to add all my favorite herbs to them and make them extra amazing. Oh yeah—I think I had this one at a street party last week . . ." and then she glided away to go sample some chocolate. Though the coincidence of the party connection was not lost on me, I was far more intrigued by her other revelation about *adding herbs* to her juice. Why had I never tried this before? In fact, aside from adding cheap beer to limeade, why had I never added *anything* to these juices?

I stopped at the store on my way home and bought bunches of parsley and mint, a burdock root, and some other produce that struck my fancy. I was so spoiled by having a plethora of ready-made juice on my hands that it had been a long time since I had actually juiced anything myself. I walked home, took my juicer off the top shelf, dusted it, and juiced the fresh produce. Of course, the mixture tasted terrible by itself. But when I mixed in some carrot-beet juice, it was suddenly divine again. Adding the herb juices actually enhanced the flavor of the original "plain" veggie juice. Amped up, I began doing more tests, emptying out some of the superfood powders I had in the cabinet, and blending them into the juice. I mixed in a little greens powder I had bought from the store made from dried, milled vegetables; incredibly, that tasted great too. Then I tried adding a couple of supplements—protein powders and herbal tinctures. Not bad at all. I realized that although the juices I worked with on a regular basis were clearly great, they stopped far short of their healthy potential. There was so much more to be done with juice!

By the end of 2008, it was time to end my four-year relationship with Portland and move back home to the sunny skies of Southern California. By this time, I was working with a couple other health food companies, and had unceremoniously passed the Juice Girl crown along to someone else. Yet, as I packed up the car with the last of my things, I knew I had to make one final stop before leaving the city: my favorite neighborhood co-op. I needed a juice.

My home kitchen today is officially one part personal juice factory. Fresh produce often spills out of the refrigerator and decorates the counter, even the stovetop—wherever there's room. The juicer has its own dedicated corner, and the compost pile never gets lonely. Lugging around produce from farmers' markets doubles as an arm workout, and it makes me happy when friends invite themselves over, not for wine or tea, but for juice. I had more volunteer taste testers for this book than I knew what to do with. I love—love—a leisurely Saturday morning, sun shining in, my sweet dog watching intently for scraps under my feet, while I press handfuls of fresh fruit, leafy greens, roots, and other produce into the juicer to make a vibrant river of flavors. There is a charge, a sensation of utter empowerment, and an overwhelming feeling of "good" about both the process and the immensely rejuvenating and delicious results.

Really, there is nothing quite like juice.

From my glass to yours,
Julie

PART ONE

JUICING FUNDAMENTALS

The superfood juicing kitchen is an inspiring one. Rigid rules and dietary dogma are replaced with healthy encouragement and aspirational choices. Everything brought into this kitchen—from the spark of new knowledge, to a restorative ingredient, to a vibrant recipe—is motivated by positive intentions. This is a kitchen of appreciation for the remedial power of superfoods and juices and all their delicious, life-changing gifts.

THE POWER OF JUICE

Juice.

Just say the word out loud: *juice.*

I mean, honestly. It even *sounds* health-giving.

We're in the midst of a true juice revolution. Juice bars are popping up right and left. And juice cleanses are becoming a common topic of conversation, whether they're shelf-stable and available at health food stores or a specialty cleanse made fresh for home delivery. In fact, the notion of "cleansing" is even replacing dieting for a growing number of people. With this uptick in popularity, one can't help but wonder, "What's in the juice?" The answer is: a lot.

When we eat, we're usually just looking to satisfy our appetite and stave off hunger—a quick sandwich here, a black-and-white cookie there. As much as two-thirds of the average North American's caloric intake is sourced from unbeneficial fats, sugar, and refined flours. When we short-change our bodies through this kind of "empty calorie" eating and deny ourselves essential nutrients, inevitably we soon feel hungry again. Ultimately, in order to feel "energized," we end up eating more calories than we need during the day. Juices, on the other hand, are at the opposite end of the spectrum: They are condensed essential nutrients in a low-calorie, liquid form, containing everything the standard American diet *lacks.* Though it may initially seem odd to think of juice as "food," anyone who is experienced in juicing will gladly (and, by no coincidence, likely energetically) tell you how remarkably sustained and content they feel after consuming a fresh-pressed beverage.

This satisfaction is largely due to easy nutrient digestion. The stomach is essentially a blender, and it requires a lot of the body's energy to break down food (just think of how lethargic you feel after a heavy meal). Not surprisingly, when you consume juice, the breakdown process is reduced dramatically, cutting the time that food stays in the stomach. Liquid nutrients are digested and absorbed more quickly, and this is why you often feel the positive effects of juices right away. Every part of the digestive process is affected: from faster digestive breakdown in the stomach, to rapid absorption into the bloodstream, to more efficient assimilation of nutrients entering cells, and even quicker elimination of toxins and waste by the colon, kidneys, and skin. In short, we become the epitome of a well-oiled machine when we regularly consume fresh juices.

Juices also give us the opportunity to enjoy many of the benefits of highly evolved diets, such as a raw food regimen or a very clean, plant-based, whole food diet, without necessarily having to commit 100%. The American Heart Association recommends a base consumption of at least 8 servings of fresh vegetables and fruits a day—a number that is easily met (or even exceeded) through solely drinking just one or two 8- to 16-ounce glasses of fresh juice. A regular inclusion of juice over a period of a few weeks can create positive changes that you can genuinely both feel and see, and even if your diet is already squeaky clean, all the additional nutrients in juices can only serve to raise your personal bar a bit higher. There's always room for a little self-improvement, right?

BENEFITS OF DRINKING RAW JUICE

Because fresh juice contains a copious amount of live enzymes, as well as bioactive vitamins and minerals, you may expect to experience at least some of these benefits, regardless of where you are on your health journey:

- Better pH balance
- Improved immune response
- Slowed aging
- Improved recovery and healing
- Cellular detoxification and cleansing
- Normalized body chemistry
- Loss of excess body fat
- More youthful skin
- Brighter eyes
- More energy
- Diminished food cravings
- Better quality sleep
- Improved mood and mental focus

UNDERSTANDING SUPERFOODS

In my work as a natural food chef and recipe developer, my cooking philosophy includes looking for the best of the best edibles, nutritionally speaking—"superfoods," as they are often called—and then experimenting with methods that make it easy to incorporate these premium food choices into our everyday lifestyles.

By "superfoods," I don't mean "weird" or "exotic" foods; nor is this just a glib marketing term. Instead, superfoods encompass a much larger dietary concept of nutrient-density, acting as the most benefit-rich foods found in nature. These are the foods that contain the greatest amount of micronutrients—vitamins, minerals, antioxidants, and phytochemicals—per calorie (in other words, helping you get the most nutritional bang out of every bite you take). However, since there are no official, legal parameters for superfood qualification, the definition itself can easily become the subject of semantic debate. For example, goji berries are undeniably a superfood (explained in detail on page 21). Jellybeans are obviously *not*. But what about pineapples? It could be argued that among their many benefits, pineapples are a wonderful whole-food source of vitamin A and C, a low-sugar fruit and a good source of bromelain, an enzyme that acts as an anti-inflammatory. Shouldn't, then, pineapples be considered a superfood? My answer may surprise you: It doesn't matter.

The word "superfood" implies a *philosophy* of

eating—it's not just a simple label to slap on a particular food or product. When you eat a superfood-infused diet you are making a conscious effort to consume foods that will deliver optimal health benefits. So, to continue the comparison between jellybeans and pineapples, it's obvious that jellybeans would never be considered a superfood because they lack any health benefit, while pineapples, on the other hand, actually confer multiple benefits, making them the clear winner of our Round One choices. Throw the hyper-condensed nutrition of goji berries into the mix, and suddenly goji berries are the clear superfood, while in comparison, pineapples would be considered simply a great natural food choice. In short, adhering to a superfood diet implies an active ideology, an underlying commitment to continually seek the best of the best, not by excluding other foods, but by bringing as many powerful, nutrient-dense foods to the table as possible (especially with a clean, whole food diet as a base).

This is why juice is so exciting: It embodies the nutrient-dense superfood philosophy by its very nature. Stripped of fillers, flours, excess sugars, oil, additives, preservatives, and so on, fresh-pressed juice is composed of pure produce. No matter how you slice it (or dice it, or squeeze it, or press it), eating an abundance of fresh produce *is* a "superfood" diet—it is benefit-rich, energy efficient eating at its finest. Truth be told, there is no quicker way to natural energy than drinking a freshly pressed juice!

RAISING THE JUICE BAR

Since juicing produce automatically elevates the level of nutrients in your diet, you might ask, why add superfoods to the mix? The answer lies in the idea of "full potential consumption." Instead of looking at a healthy diet as one of restriction, adopt an opportunistic attitude: Every time you sit down to eat, it's an opportunity to consume something that's not only delicious (of course!), but *also* an opportunity to gain peak nutrition. Many fresh-pressed juice recipes—both homemade and commercial—can fall short from a health-giving standpoint, often due to the juice's potential perks being "watered down" by the use of large amounts of less nutritious produce (or worse, refined sugars), which offer limited benefits in comparison to superfood ingredients.

So while there's absolutely nothing wrong with a glass of straight fresh-pressed apple or carrot juice now and then, the truth is nature has much more to offer us. *A whole lot more.* Why not take advantage of this bounty and catapult the nutritional value of the juice you drink into a beautiful elixir that has a phenomenally broad spectrum of health benefits? It's so easy to turn a healthy juice into the ultimate revitalizing drink just though the addition of superfoods. From a health perspective, it's the difference between being financially stable and being unbelievably rich . . . which is why this book is packed with 100 delicious, inspirational recipes to help you achieve the incredible "healthfully wealthy" experience, through the simple, smart use of superfoods.

JUICING WITH SUPERFOODS

I love the ritual of juicing.

It starts with shopping for food, where I love filling my basket with a gargantuan pile of fresh produce and feeling a sense of pride holding its beauty . . . a rainbow in the form of a colorful fruit bouquet, quite deserving of admiration by my fellow shoppers.

At home, I love displaying that beautiful bounty on the counter as I assemble the ingredients to make a juice recipe, coupled with a proud moment of realization: "Yes—oh yes—I'm going to consume *all that*." I love the methodical "feeding" of produce into the machine, the precious liquid flowing out into the collecting cup in colorful streams. And finally—at last!—I love the frothy pour of the most vibrantly energetic fresh beverage ever, one that's absolutely bursting with life and begging to be consumed. Sometimes, I even pour my juice into a wine glass, as a reminder that what I'm sipping is something extremely special that should be savored consciously (and that I should not let my overeager taste buds get the better of me and polish it off as if in a drinking contest. Please affirm I'm not the only one who does this?). Juicing is deeply fulfilling on so many levels, and once you begin to practice keeping a self-loving, nutritional intention in mind, the instinctual positivity that develops will ensure you never look back.

SUPERFOOD JUICING PRINCIPLES

Before going any further into the exciting world of superfood juicing, there are a few ground rules to keep in mind, setting the stage for the most nutritionally beneficial alchemy possible:

1 Buy organic.

In general, buying organic produce is a smart move for many reasons: It saves you from consuming pesticides, herbicides, fungicides, and various chemicals, many of which can be dangerous to your health. Choosing organic is also an environmentally friendly move, supporting farming practices that use natural growing methods as opposed to ones that contribute to the industrial, chemical soup that is poured into the world every day. In juicing, choosing organic produce is more important than ever, as not only is the entire fruit or vegetable (including the skin) often used, but these foods are consumed in relatively large quantities. Don't undermine the health and cleansing benefits of juicing by ingesting a concentrated sludge of pesticides. Remember: Keep it organic, and keep your body (and the earth!) clean.

2 Save sugar for dessert.

Reducing sugar is an important concept in my book *Superfood Smoothies*, but to be honest, it's even more important when applied to juicing. Nobody wants to be a tyrant about sugar (let alone listen to one), and even if you're eating a clean, whole food, plant-based diet rich in fresh produce, there is certainly a time and place to enjoy a little decadence now and then—it's called dessert. (Of course desserts, too, can be made using minimal amounts of sugar and far healthier sweeteners.) However, the only way to really justify having dessert is to eliminate unnecessary additives (including sugar in its multiple forms) from the food you eat during the rest of the day. Where most people get into trouble with sugar is usually not the one cupcake they enjoyed at a friend's house or the cookie they had at work. Rather, the real problem lies in the *accrual* of sugars found in drinks, sauces, salad dressings, soups, snacks, nutrition bars, you name it, that deviously add up over the course of the day.

Cutting out sugar is even more important in juices because of the inherent nature of this kind of food. Through the pressing process of the produce, the "bulk" is stripped away, meaning that the fiber, fat, and protein, which is concentrated in the pulp, is lost. So while all the plant-based vitamins, minerals, antioxidants, and phytochemicals are beneficially saturated in juices, natural sugars will be higher too. Additionally, since there are no other macronutrients outside of carbohydrates (and fiber-free carbohydrates at that) to slow down digestion, everything encapsulated within the juice is released into the bloodstream at a faster rate. Therefore, the body can digest apple juice like a turbo-boost version of eating a few whole apples.

For most people, this digestive amplification is not a problem in moderation (if you are concerned

with blood sugar levels, see page 52 on how to use chia seeds to slow down the release of sugar). However, if we *add* sugar to the natural sugars that are already in fresh-pressed juice, it's easy to understand why this sets the stage for elevating blood sugar far too high, creating a true (and undesirable) "sugar rush." If you want a sweeter juice than your fresh ingredients create, I recommend taking a more nature-made approach by simply using more fruit before reaching for the sugar (or agave nectar, or, even healthier, coconut sugar). While you're still adding "sugar," it's a far superior and much more beneficial choice than any form of refined sugar. Even better? Try using a healthy, natural, sugar-free option like stevia. For more on sweetening your juice without adding additional sugars, see page 57.

3 **Buy from farmers' markets.**
This isn't necessarily a steadfast rule, since many conventional markets offer superb produce, rather more of a helpful tip. Farmers' markets offer some of the freshest produce available. It's sourced locally and sometimes even sold at discounted prices. You can also find different varieties of common produce, such as heirloom purple carrots and golden beets, or less-common leafy greens like mizuna. On my last trip to my local farmers' market, I found kumquats that were the length of my thumb and tasted like a sweet, zesty marmalade—a rare edible gem with such immense, playful flavor! Rotating your produce with some of these "specialty" items not only keeps your homemade juices continually evolving and interesting, it also offers a rainbow of nutrient nuances that are available only by mixing things up.

4 **Lean on vegetables (and low-sugar fruits).**
There are many fruit-juice recipes in this book that are a true pleasure to savor and supply a treasure trove of nutrients as well. Nevertheless, if you're looking to consume large quantities of juice throughout the day, be sure to incorporate a healthy mix of green juices and root vegetable juices as well. Consuming some fruit juice is beneficial, but more than a couple servings can be too high in (natural) sugars for some people. From a health perspective, vegetables and low-sugar fruits are always the best choice.

5 **Include superfoods.**
Yes! The golden rule of this book is: Increase the nutritional potential of juice through the use of superfoods. Look to juice as a supplier of incredible nutrient-dense foods. Even if you're just having orange juice, "spike it" with a little camu berry powder for extra vitamin C, or mix in a small spoonful of wheatgrass powder to boost the detoxification properties and incorporate a little undetectable "green." Look at every juice as an opportunity, a call to action to benefit a little more with the easy addition of superfoods. The recipes in this book will show you how.

THE ARCHITECTURE OF A SUPERFOOD JUICE

If the ground rules for making the most nutritionally beneficial (and delicious) juices seem relatively lax to you, good! They are. But the *best* news is that creating an "ultimate superfood juice" is even easier. Successful juice recipes are broken down into four structural elements: base ingredients, add-ons, superfoods, and flavor balancers. Master this basic design concept and you are well on your way to making your very own mind-blowing, celebratory new concoctions!

BASE INGREDIENTS

After making just a few juice recipes, you will quickly discover that all juices are comprised of one or two core ingredients—specific produce that makes up around 70% (sometimes more!) of the juice and makes up the "filler," or base, of the recipe. You'll also notice these base ingredients are used over and over in recipes, for several reasons. First, these ingredients are palate-pleasing simply on their own, which cannot be said for every vegetable, or even every fruit. Sweet carrots, for example, are a far cry from bitter burdock root. Second, base ingredients often contain a large proportion of water in relation to bulk, which yields higher quantities of juice. Lastly, the base ingredients for recipes in this book are relatively inexpensive, and keep down the overall cost of juicing. Consider the following list of base ingredients. As long as you have one or two of them on hand, you will always be able to make a delicious-tasting fresh juice.

Apples and Pears

Few people in the world don't like fresh-pressed apple or pear juice. Using just one or two of these fruits in conjunction with a selection of more nutritious produce creates almost instant palatability. The fresher the apple or pear (think farmers' markets and seasonal varieties), the better the sweetness and flavor of the resulting juice, as apples become more mellow with time. In addition to being complementary to just about any fruit juice combination, these fruits can also be used very successfully with vegetable juices, and are a wonderful match for green juices too. (Note that after about an hour, juices made with apples and pears will begin to darken, as their browning enzymes are activated by exposure to oxygen.)

Prep notes Although most juicers are equipped to filter out hard seeds, apples and pears should be cored (or at least seeded) before juicing the fruit to avoid any risk of exposure to arsenic, a natural toxin that is contained in the seeds.

Celery

Aromatic, watery, and fibrous, celery's rich mineral content gives it a "saltiness," and when juiced, provides a savory flavor. Used as a base ingredient, celery tastes best in green drinks and vegetable drinks, though it can also be used in smaller quantities as an add-on in fruit beverages to help balance flavor.

Prep notes From the base to the leaves, the entire celery stalk may (and should!) be used, with the exception of the last half-inch on the root end, which often harbors dirt and should be trimmed. Note that celery leaves tend to impart a stronger flavor than the stalk.

Cucumbers

Cucumbers are the lightest base ingredient you can use, as well as the lowest in calories, sodium, and sugar. Although their flavor is subtle, water-rich cucumbers provide a large quantity of juice, and are profoundly hydrating. They are one of my favorite base ingredients, best used in green drinks and vegetable drinks.

Prep notes Much of the cucumber's nutrition is found in the skin, so if you're using organic, simply wash the cucumber thoroughly before juicing and use the whole thing. If you're using conventionally grown cucumbers, peel before using to avoid waxes and concentrated pesticides on the exterior.

Melons

(Watermelons, Cantaloupes, Honeydews)

A botanical relative to cucumbers, melons are as watery as fruit gets, and adding any variety of melon to juice makes for a popular treat. Juicing them alone brings out a melon's cucumber flavor, but when used in conjunction with other fruit or sweeteners, their distinctive flavor really comes alive. Melons can be used with both fruit juices and green juices as a base.

Prep notes For the sweetest, purest-flavored, and best-tasting juice, scoop out the seeds and cut away the hard rind before juicing. Melons with thinner skins, like watermelon or honeydew, may be juiced with their rinds still intact if organic. Micronutrients concentrated in some melon skin confer a raft of health benefits. Watermelon rind, for example, contains large amounts of a phytonutrient called citrulline, which the body converts into arginine to promote a healthy heart, improve circulation, support the immune system, and, reportedly, it can even work as effectively as Viagra. Needless to say, as strange as it may seem, consider juicing the rind!

Pineapples

Though it is on the costlier side in comparison to other base ingredients, sweet and tropical-tasting pineapple juice can easily be considered an exotic cocktail all on its own. Pineapple is an excellent source of bromelain, an enzyme that is well known for its anti-inflammatory properties, and can also help with digestion. The versatile sweet and slightly acidic flavor of pineapple is a welcome base for fruit and green juices, and may be used as a complementary background ingredient in root juices as well.

Prep notes Although it is safe to run a pineapple rind through your juicer, the skin does tend to make the juice taste a little bitter. Most commonly the rind is cut off, along with the spiky frond at the top of the pineapple. The core of the pineapples, on the other hand, which is usually discarded due to its tough texture, can and should be juiced along with the rest of the fruit.

Sweet Citrus Fruits
(Oranges, Tangerines, Grapefruits)

The sweet-tart juice of citrus fruit is wonderfully variable and can even be juiced without a machine, making it perhaps the most popular of all produce to juice. So, it should come as no surprise that these fruits are among the most important ones to include in juices. What sets "freshly juiced" apart from the average OJ-in-a-bottle has to do with the method of juicing. Most citrus is juiced by pressing out the nectar of the pigmented inner sections only; yet there is much more potential in citrus fruit than meets the eye! Despite its sometimes bitter taste when eaten whole (which is why it is often avoided), the spongy white pith and the inner skin that separates the segments is rather mild in flavor in juice form. It's also a good source of blood-pressure lowering flavonoids, and makes the juice a little frothier, too. When using organic varieties, the peel can sometimes be used to give juice an especially bright flavor via its intensely aromatic oils, but it should be used in moderation to avoid becoming overpowering. Oranges are more versatile than grapefruits thanks to their sweetness, but both are welcome components for fruit and even root juices. From a flavor-pairing standpoint, most sweet citrus is less conducive as a base for green drinks, but it can be used in conjunction with celery in milder blends.

Prep notes Unless otherwise noted, the recipes in this book call for peeled citrus fruits for a more balanced flavor, though some peel can always be added to taste. The white pith is a welcome addition and may be included as desired. Most juicers strain out and discard the seeds, so there is little reason to remove them ahead of time.

Sweet Roots
(Carrots, Beets, and Parsnips)

Vegetable sweetness at its finest, these colorful roots offer nutrient-rich sugars and a soothing milkiness, and blend well with both vegetable and fruit juices. An inexpensive base option, root vegetables have long been a favorite ingredient at juice bars, and offer rich amounts of antioxidants, vitamins, and minerals.

Prep notes Most people prefer to use just the root, but if the produce is organic and very fresh, the leaves may be cleaned thoroughly and used as well, providing extra chlorophyll and a "green" flavor (beet greens are a favorite). For the maximum nutrition, roots need only to be scrubbed well and not peeled (recommended), since the highest concentration of nutrients is in the skin. However, for a sweeter flavor, remove some (or all) of the peel before juicing.

Sweet Tubers and Hard Squash
(Jicama, Yams, Sweet Potatoes, Pumpkin)

Surprisingly successful juices can be made from these bulbous treasures. Because of their high starch content, it's a good idea to combine them with other base ingredients in juices for easier digestion. Both tubers and squash offer a sweetness and frothy richness that makes an ideal base to support warming spices, nut and seed blends, and even protein powders.

Prep notes Organic yams, sweet potatoes, and even winter squash may be simply scrubbed clean and juiced with their nutritious skins intact. For jicama, note that the skin is often brushed with wax for easier peeling, and if this is the case, you will need to peel the jicama before cutting it into chunks for juicing, so the wax does not clog your juicer. If a sweeter flavor is desired, tubers may be peeled first, but as these types of skins are not "processed" into juice very well by the machine, the difference in flavor and nutrition for peeling versus non-peeling is small.

ADD-ONS

Add-ons represent a vast collection of fruits and vegetables that are wonderfully nutritious and flavorful, but are not quite as nutritionally dense as ingredients that have "superfood" status. "Add-ons" should not be considered base ingredients because they are at their best when added in smaller quantities. The drawbacks of using these ingredients on their own as a juice include a diminished yield, higher cost, and/or a stronger flavor. Nevertheless, the possibilities for ingredients in this category are virtually endless, since the underlying theme of the recipes in this book is: If it grows out of the ground, you can juice it! Even more excitingly, every add-on comes with its own characteristic social security number of vitamins, minerals, antioxidants, and phytochemical benefits. Just because it doesn't have the status of "superfood fancy-pants," doesn't mean it's not incredibly healthy—all the more reason to enjoy diversity and abundance. Variety is truly key to long-term health.

Here are some of the main add-on ingredients that are used in this book. By no means should you feel limited by this list. Experiment!

Bell Peppers
Burdock Root
Grapes
Mangoes
Papayas
Peas
Radishes
Rhubarb Stalks
Stone Fruits (peaches, plums, apricots, cherries, and so on)
Summer Squash
Tomatoes

REDUCING THE COST OF INGREDIENTS

Drinking fresh juice is akin to putting premium gas in your car, except with juice, that investment is in *you* . . . in your longevity, quality of life, and well-being. After all, you have just one body to last a lifetime, and it deserves the very best fuel to run on. If you've ever ordered a glass of fine wine at a restaurant without hesitation, you should have no qualms about the cost of making an exquisite, fresh-pressed, life-giving juice. It's simply a matter of perspective: When you consider the value of the foods that nourish the very cells of your being (and, ultimately, how affordable it is to pay for them), slashing the budget of this form of "health care" does not look like a good idea!

Nevertheless, I don't like spending excess money on groceries any more than you do. Therefore, the recipes in this book call for ingredients that make the most sense in terms of accessibility and cost. For example, although you could juice fresh pomegranate seeds (and oh my, is it ever a phenomenon of tasty pleasure!), most home juicers are simply not equipped to press pomegranates as efficiently as their commercial counterparts, and the yield is a disappointingly small amount of juice from a fairly expensive piece of fruit. For this reason, adding purchased pomegranate juice to fresh-pressed mixes is a more rational approach, and one that I embrace. I've made sure to do all the homework ahead of time so you can get the most bang for your buck when it comes to sourcing premium superfood ingredients for the recipes in this book.

Most brands of packaged organic super-foods (powders, seeds, etc.) enjoy a long shelf life, and generally cost about the same at various retailers, so other than being on the hunt for special sales and "deals" whenever possible, there is little room in this arena for jaw-dropping cost-saving tips. Rather, looking to cut the cost of *fresh* produce ingredients (ones that need to be purchased regularly) is significantly more effective.

Apply the tricks below and you can save a tremendous amount of money over the long run, especially for those of you who are regular juicers:

SHOP AT FARMERS' MARKETS.

I've found that the cost of produce at my local farmers' market varies from being about the same as the grocery store up to as much as 50% less, depending on the season. If you become a regular customer and get to know the vendors at your farmers' market, you may even get extra discounts (or even a few freebies) from time to time. You may also find that the farmers' market fruits and vegetables are often bigger and fresher than the produce at your local grocery store.

BUY IN BULK.

While this doesn't apply to everything you may want to buy, it makes sense to purchase some items in large quantities. Big bags of carrots, apples, sweet potatoes, and citrus fruits are often sold at a remarkably reduced cost and will last a couple of weeks. Plus, buying bulk quantities of produce is simply an incentive to juice more often, so that nothing goes to waste!

AVOID PREPARED PRODUCE.

Many grocery stores offer precut fruits and vegetables as a shortcut for cooking and snacking. Three words: Don't do it. You pay a seriously heavy extra cost for the luxury of buying, say, presliced apples and jicama, or already-cubed melons and pineapple. You can even buy containers of pomegranate seeds at top dollar. But juicing requires such large amounts of produce, you'll end up forking over a small fortune for the convenience of precut veggies and fruit. Plus, you'll likely find the already-prepared produce (and resulting juice) is not as fresh and flavorful as when you do the prep immediately before juicing. Invest in the few extra minutes it takes to cut up your own produce, and reap the savings.

USE SEASONAL INGREDIENTS.

I once paid $7 for the privilege of purchasing a single pomegranate in July. (Don't let this happen to you!) Instead, enjoy juice blends that utilize the freshest produce of the season. If you're not sure what's in season, here's a hint: It's primarily the stuff that's on sale. Apples are usually inexpensive in colder months, while cucumbers are often a fraction of their regular cost in the summer. Feel free to substitute the ingredients in juice blends with interesting seasonal counterparts. Swapping out winter-friendly kale and replacing it with crisp lettuce during the summer is a great solution, or toggle between parsnips and jicama during the cold versus warm times of the year. In fact, one of the best methods to achieve a sustainable juicing lifestyle is to continually switch up your produce and enjoy the maximum health benefits offered through variety of nutrients and flavors. Keeping a seasonal focus makes sense on every level.

SUPERFOODS

Think of superfoods as your top-shelf ingredients, nutritionally speaking. Although you won't be using more than a little bit of them at a time, they are the key to taking any juice to the next level of concentrated rewards. Now, unless you're already well stocked with superfoods, or are especially eager to jump into the superfood lifestyle full speed ahead (and I can't say I blame you), there is no need to run to the store and buy every superfood on this list. Start slow, aim to incorporate a couple new superfoods a month, and remember there's nothing wrong with substituting or leaving out ingredients from any of the juice recipes in this book; it's easy to swap in blueberries instead of goji berries, for example, while still getting a fantastic superfood juice in the bargain. The benefits of folding these amazing new ingredients into your juicing is nothing short of revolutionary.

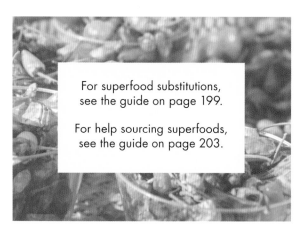

For superfood substitutions, see the guide on page 199.

For help sourcing superfoods, see the guide on page 203.

✳ SUPER GREENS

Unsure of where to begin in the realm of adding superfoods into your life? Start with leafy greens. We all know eating more green vegetables is the key to next-level health, but most of us don't sit down to an 8-cup spinach salad a couple times a day. Yet with juicing, you *can*. Easily. By extracting the fiber and pressing out only the condensed nutrition of greens, you can consume enormous quantities of them, and as often as you like. Personally, I can attest to the healing power of greens: My skin never looks so radiant and my eyes are never clearer as when I am drinking green juice on a regular basis . . . and that's just an exterior benefit (although it is a clue to a very happy interior). Many of the remarkable advantages of greens are best preserved when they are consumed in a raw form, making juicing the perfect catalyst for leafy green consumption. Hold a green juice up to the light—is anything more magically vivid? With such pleasant flavors and welcome energizing benefits, it is almost a guarantee you will come to truly *crave* this level of peak health.

Varieties The most common varieties of juice-friendly greens include lettuces (especially crunchier varieties like romaine), kale, chard, bok choy, and the most mild-tasting of all greens, spinach. Other greens, such as watercress, arugula, purslane, broccoli, cabbage, dandelion greens, and local varieties may be used too, although smaller quantities are recommended, since they will usually impart a stronger, more bitter flavor. If fresh greens are unavailable, a spoonful of "greens powder" made of dehydrated vegetables is a good second choice. You can find greens powders in natural food stores and sometimes in the supplement sections of larger grocery stores.

Benefits There's very good reason "green drinks" are often considered such a go-to health tool. Green vegetables are the only way to infuse chlorophyll, the green-pigmented antioxidant found in plants, into your diet. In fact, leafy greens have the highest concentration of chlorophyll of all mature land plants. Chlorophyll aids in creating a healthy alkaline body (it balances biological pH), it is a premium detoxifier, and it helps blood cells deliver oxygen. Green leafy vegetables are produce "gold" because they are abundant in just about every micronutrient you could desire, including minerals of all varieties, vitamins, and protective antioxidants. The darker the green color, the greater the benefits!

Prep notes Wash greens thoroughly to remove any grit so that it doesn't get into the finished juice. Crispier produce creates more juice, so always use the entirety of crunchy stalks and stems. If you're using a centrifugal juicer, see page 32 for techniques on how to maximize the yield.

✳ GRASSES AND SPROUTS

Grasses and sprouts are, essentially, baby versions of leafy greens, and are similar in benefits: alkalizing, cleansing, low in calories and sugars,

and high in essential minerals like magnesium and vitamins like C and A. Interestingly, a plant's nutrition does not necessarily increase in proportion to its mature size. Full-grown radishes, for example, contain 27mg of calcium per 100g, whereas 100g of radish sprouts contain 57mg of calcium. This signifies that little sprouts actually have a greater nutrient density (higher levels of micronutrients per calorie) than mature vegetables, which is why they are such an incredible superfood.

Varieties Any vegetable is a sprout or grass at some time, but some varieties are more palatable than others for juicing. Seek sprouts like clover and alfalfa, which have a delicious, mild flavor. Mung bean sprouts are also exceptionally good to use because of their high water content. Wheatgrass and barley grass are the most popular forms of grasses to juice, and may be used interchangeably and either juiced fresh, or used in a powder form and stirred in.

Benefits Sprouts and grasses are a tremendously good source of vitamins, including A, C, and K; they abound in minerals like calcium and iron; and they are highly alkalizing, which can stabilize an unbalanced body pH and promote a healthy homeostasis. The nutrition in alfalfa sprouts can aid in the fight against an array of conditions, including infections and even cancer, as well as normalizing estrogen production and encouraging blood clotting. Wheatgrass and barley grass are particularly effective detoxifiers due to their impressive chlorophyll content. They can help normalize the thyroid for a balanced metabolism, and are ideal ingredients for a wide variety of cleanses. The nutritional value of 3 pounds of wheatgrass is comparable to as much as 70 pounds of vegetables!

Prep notes The sole downside to using fresh sprouts and grasses is that most juicers—unless they are specifically designed for these kinds of greens—cannot efficiently process such delicate produce. Running a handful of broccoli sprouts through a traditional centrifugal juicer will result in a microscopic juice yield that will quickly make you wish you had chosen to simply eat a sprout salad and put this book through the juicer instead. If juicing with fresh sprouts and grasses is something you desire, I highly recommended you use a dedicated "wheatgrass juicer" that is equipped to handle the task (see page 203 for sourcing). Otherwise, use powdered varieties like wheatgrass powder, or a greens mix that includes various dehydrated and milled sprouts (see page 203 for powder sources). The recipes in this book call for only wheatgrass powder (never fresh juice), but you may substitute as desired. *One serving of grass powder (serving size varies from brand to brand) usually equals about one ounce of fresh juice.*

※ ALGAE

Even the smallest addition of culinary algae can quickly catapult the most mundane juice into one that can claim true superfood status, thanks to the incredible potency and life-giving nutrition of these gems from the sea. Algae are ancient organisms, celebrated for their staggering potential to heal, and, of all known foods, are the most condensed sources of chlorophyll.

Varieties The most commonly sold varieties of green and blue-green algae are chlorella and spirulina. Though they can be used interchangeably most of the time, I recommend the use of spirulina over chlorella in this book because it has a significantly milder taste. Regardless of the variety of algae you choose, look for pure, powdered forms that do not contain fillers. If purchasing chlorella, make a note to buy a "broken cell wall" variety that ensures digestibility through a special processing technique.

Benefits Because they are so rich in chlorophyll, algae are natural detoxifiers that can even help eliminate heavy metals like lead or mercury from the body. An arsenal of vitamins (including the elusive plant-based B-12), minerals (spirulina has 28 times more iron than beef liver), and even high-quality protein, make the healing potential of these ingredients truly amazing. Recent discoveries have linked regular algae consumption with reduced risk of cancers, heightened immune activity, increased energy, and effective detoxification. When it comes to the health properties of this special group of superfoods, the list genuinely goes on and on.

Prep notes Alga often has a strong "sea" flavor—part of the reason why it is often sold in capsule form (for those that would rather "take" and not "eat" it). Yet the flavor is easily masked, as you'll discover with the recipes in this book that use powdered forms of spirulina and chlorella. You can always use more of these powders than the recipe calls for, but take note that they are very powerful superfoods, both in nutrition and in flavor. You'll want to blend these recipes especially well, as a juice disrupted with algae clumps is no one's friend.

✳ FRESH HERBS

Because their power to heal is so potent, many herbs teeter between the classification of "superfoods" and bona fide natural medicine. In the context of juicing, I count fresh green leafy herbs as superfoods because these herbs can be used in a sizeable quantity without overwhelming the body.

Varieties Though there are many types of culinary herbs, the recipes in this book focus on more common, juice-friendly varieties such as mint, parsley, and cilantro. Experimental use of other fresh herbs is absolutely encouraged.

Benefits Like other green leafy vegetables, herbs provide good sources of chlorophyll, making them both pH-balancing and cleansing foods. In addition to their impressive vitamin and mineral load, herbs are known for a powerful set of phytochemicals that contain effective medicinal, anti-viral, anti-bacterial, anti-inflammatory, and anti-cancer properties. Parsley, for example, contains a concentrated substance called apigenin, a promising breast-cancer fighting compound,

while fresh mint is a known effective herbal treatment for nausea. Herbs have a long history of use in healing, so be sure to include them in your juices whenever possible.

Prep notes Green herbs can be juiced in their entirety, stem and all. If you're using a centrifugal juicer, be sure to tightly bundle the herbs and wrap them in a large leaf, like romaine lettuce or kale, to get the maximum amount of juice from these delicate superfoods.

✳ NORTH AMERICAN SUPER-BERRIES

Oh, the varieties! Who isn't enamored with a juicy strawberry or sweet-tart blackberry? Using fresh berries in juices is tremendously rewarding and creates delicate flavor magic that simply cannot be replicated by extracts or commercial varieties. Berries in general—the edible variety, that is— are among nature's most potent fruit superfoods, and some of the most delicious as well.

Varieties All common berry varieties, such as blueberries, strawberries, blackberries, raspberries, and cranberries, make exceptional additions to juices. Feel free to experiment with more localized specialty berries, such as fresh gooseberries, mulberries, and huckleberries, if they're available.

Benefits Every berry comes with its own unique collection of incredible micronutrient gifts, but in general, berries are usually very good providers of vitamins. Almost all berries are particularly high in vitamin C and often vitamin A, along with

many of the vitamin B complex, and sometimes even vitamin E. They can provide some minerals as well (though usually not at the elite level of vegetables and roots), and are good sources of anti-aging antioxidants with high ORAC scores (scores that measure antioxidant levels), and anti-inflammatory phytochemicals. Studies continue to pour in on the widespread benefits of berries: One study recently showed strawberries to boost red blood cells' response to oxidative stress, while cranberries are a known natural tool to prevent urinary tract infections.

Prep notes Because fresh berries are so delicate and often rather expensive to buy at the market, the freeze-thaw method, outlined on page 20 (which uses frozen berries), is highly recommended for maximum juice yield and reduced cost. One exception is strawberries, which juice very nicely fresh and can have their leaves and stems included—just be sure to use the lowest, gentlest setting on your machine to ensure the largest juicy output.

❋ PREMIUM SUPER-BERRIES

While all edible berries are beneficial and worthy of "superfood" status, some berries stand out even further as extra health-giving. Many of these "super-berries" are still considered "exotic" underdogs, at least in North American markets. But, as our knowledge of the world's most amazing natural foods continues to expand, the scene is changing. Now, many of these super-berries, from areas all around the world, are making their way into the limelight, and have begun to peek out of the shelves of even the most unassuming grocery stores. The health benefits of these special varieties are not only celebrated in historical and popular narratives, but also in the pages of the most prestigious science journals as well. So, although some varieties of super-berries may be unfamiliar, their profound nourishment, impressive flavors, and rejuvenating potential make them an exciting addition to juices. In the pages that follow, you will find a list of these remarkable berries—treasures that have been lovingly tucked into many of the recipes in this book. (For help with sourcing, see page 203). I invite you to enjoy them!

Acai Berries

These deep purple gems grow in clusters on the tall açai palm, found in the Amazon. Here, the colorful berries are collected, pressed into a pulpy juice, and usually enjoyed in beverage form. Acai juice is rich-tasting due to its content of healthy monounsaturated fats (rare for a berry), which, coupled with a remarkable level of antioxidants, make it a sought-after berry for energy, stamina, skin health, and heart health.

Prep notes Though acai is increasingly available as a prepackaged juice, this form is not recommended for the recipes in this book, as most store brands include additional sugar in their blends. Instead, use freeze-dried acai powder, which is the most shelf-stable, cost-effective, and pure form of acai currently available in North America as it contains *just* acai. (It is also the most versatile form for use in recipes other than juices; try mixing a spoonful into cooked oatmeal . . . yum!) To achieve a creamy, smooth texture and fully incorporate acai's rich oils, use a blender to mix acai powder with a base juice. Store unused acai powder in the refrigerator or freezer to extend its shelf life.

Aronia Berries

While dark purple aronia berries come from a common shrub that Native Americans often used as food, aronia is only just beginning its journey into superfood stardom in our modern-day diet. Like maqui and acai, aronia berries offer exceedingly high levels of anthocyanin antioxidants, which enhance circulation and help fight diseases caused by oxidation (like some forms of cancer). Because aronia berries are quite tart naturally (earning them the alternate name "chokeberry"), they are best suited for fresh-pressed fruit juices, which can give them a sweet boost.

Prep notes Aronia berries are sometimes available in frozen and even fresh forms in some North American markets. I strongly encourage you to grab these berries wherever and however you find them! However, for the few recipes in this book that include aronia as an ingredient,

JUICING BERRIES

Although the undeniable benefits of a plant-based diet are becoming more widely celebrated, I still often meet people who challenge me with the notion that they just "don't like superfoods . . . and won't eat them." To this, I usually smile and retort with a sly question,

"Do you like strawberries?"

And to date, the response has universally been, "Yes, of course!"

"Well, then," I reply, "you like superfoods."

Leaving semantics at the door, it's far easier to focus on the beautiful, simple, and robust-flavored plant-based bounty we can enjoy from superfoods in all their delicious permutations, and berries are a perfect example of this. Just about everyone likes berries, even young children! But despite their mass appeal, fresh berries are quite expensive since you need such large quantities of them to create a single serving. So, the question isn't whether consuming berries provides a healthy lift, but is it worth juicing them?

It can be. Strawberries are the most successful in terms of juicing because of their large size, high water content, and stronger structure. Meanwhile more delicate berries (like raspberries), require a very different method to best extract the maximum amount of juice, avoid waste, and reduce cost. To most efficiently incorporate berries into a juice at home, it actually makes the most sense to use them in a frozen form than fresh, which is substantially less expensive. Here's how to do it:

FREEZE-THAW BERRY JUICING METHOD

The freeze-thaw method is very useful for creating juice from berries because, during the freezing process, the ice crystals that form inside of the fruit poke holes through its cellular structure, allowing much of the juice to seep out when the berries have thawed. As a result, using this method will create a much higher juice yield than simply pressing fresh berries.

You will need:

1 package frozen berries (a variety of your choice)

1 medium bowl

1 large piece of cheesecloth, at least twice the size of the bowl's interior surface area

Directions:

Fold the cheesecloth to create a double layer, and lay it inside the bowl. Pour the frozen berries on top of the cheesecloth, and place the bowl in the refrigerator. Allow the frozen berries to thaw completely for several hours or overnight. Once the berries are fully thawed, collect the edges of the cheesecloth to form a bag, then use your hands to gently squeeze and "milk" out the juice through the cloth into the bowl. The resulting berry juice may be mixed into recipes as desired.

TIP Excess berry pulp can be sweetened slightly or used as is and enjoyed as a fresh raw jam. It will keep for two to three days, if refrigerated.

I suggest using the more accessible form of pre-pressed aronia juice instead of the costlier and less accessible berries. (For information about where to find aronia products see page 203.)

Camu Berries

Another South American superstar, the camu berry tastes a bit like a cranberry. It's reddish pink, extremely tart, and very potent. Camu is the most concentrated source of vitamin C of any known food; one teaspoon contains almost 1200% RDA of the vitamin. In other words, you would need to consume about 8½ oranges just to match the vitamin content of a single teaspoon of camu berry powder. Although camu doesn't taste particularly good on its own, so little of it is needed to catapult the vitamin C content of a juice that it can be added to virtually any kind of fresh beverage. A bonus: Vitamin C is a natural preservative, so adding a pinch of camu berry powder to fresh juices can help extend and preserve their delicate nutrition!

Prep notes In South America, camu berries are often pressed into fresh juice—a health elixir, which, unfortunately, has yet to penetrate markets in North America. For the recipes in this book, I recommend a freeze-dried powder form of camu berry. It does not need to be refrigerated, and because the powder is so concentrated and portion sizes so miniscule, even a small bag will last an extremely long time. This small serving size also makes this superfood ingredient easy to either add into (or leave out of) virtually any recipe.

Goji Berries

Known as the "longevity berry" in China, goji berries have played an important role in Chinese medicine for thousands of years. An extremely balanced food, goji berries are especially high in carotene, and contain all major macronutrients (even protein), as well as over 20 vitamins and minerals. They have been shown to be particularly supportive of the immune system (including cancer prevention and treatment), eye health, and memory.

Prep notes Whole goji berries are usually available at the market in various forms: sun-dried (like a raisin), a freeze-dried powder, and a pure juice. The recipes in this book feature dried goji berries as they're the most widely available, but any form can be substituted and used effectively. Since the entire goji berry is of such great healing value, dried goji berries are best incorporated into fresh-pressed juices in two ways: steeping in the juice like a tea (and leaving in the resulting plumped, hydrated berries as textural goodies), or using a fresh-pressed juice as a base and blending the goji berries in after (straining the juice, if desired).

In general, two tablespoons dried goji berries = one tablespoon goji berry powder = one ounce goji berry juice.

Maqui Berries

A common fruit that is domestically grown and wild-crafted in Patagonia (a stunning region of southern Chile), maqui berries are widely renowned for their delicious flavor and intensely violet pigment. Like a rainforest version of a blueberry, these small fruits may have a familiar berry flavor, yet their benefits are anything but ordinary. Maqui berries are the number one antioxidant-dense fruit tested in the world, due to their phenomenally high purple antioxidants, known as anthocyanins. A topic of increasing scientific interest, anthocyanins have been shown to have many positive effects on the body, including increased blood circulation and decreased inflammation, and act as a potent anti-aging nutrient.

Prep notes Although fresh maqui berries are a ubiquitous sight in areas of southern Chile and occasionally it is possible to find maqui berry juice in North America, the most commonly available form, and the best for juices, is freeze-dried maqui berry powder. Shelf-stable and extremely potent, it does not take much more than a spoonful of maqui berry powder to enhance a juice . . . and turn it purple as well! Maqui powder is water soluble, so no blending is required, nor does it need to be refrigerated; simply keep it in a cool, dry, dark place.

Sea Buckthorn Berries

Although this orange berry does not come from the sea like its name suggests, it does prefer growing along coastal areas, especially in Asia and Europe. Tart and slightly sweet, the taste of this complex-flavored fruit includes background notes of lemon and honey. The edible seeds of the sea buckthorn berry can be refined into a medicinal oil, while the fruit, in its entirety, offers additional nutritional promise with its high concentration of vitamins A and C, anti-inflammatory antioxidants, and even the highly elusive (and newly studied) omega-7 essential fatty acids, which promote tissue regeneration and skin health.

Prep notes Sea buckthorn is difficult to harvest and delicate to ship, making it a rare sight in most markets in whole form. For the recipes in this book, use a prepressed sea buckthorn berry juice, available in many natural supplement stores (or see page 203 for online ordering). You will need only a little bit of it to mix into the recipes to reap the benefits, and sea buckthorn's pleasant tart flavor is a beautifully unique addition to fruit juices or even some vegetable juices, or wherever a citrus note is welcome.

✳ SUPER-FRUITS

Every edible fruit in nature has genuine value to offer in the balance of a healthy diet. Yet there are several kinds of fruit that stand out from the rest because of the very high concentration of nutrition they offer. In this section of "super-fruits," you will find some of the most health-promising options that can be included to make truly unique juice recipes.

Mangosteen

Between its complex flavor, which can vary in taste from peach to strawberry to vanilla, and the creamy, thick juice it creates, it's easy to see why mangosteen is an extra-attractive superfood. In fact, this dark purple fruit, with its white, fleshy interior, is so popular in Southeast Asia, where it is grown, that it is sometimes regally referred to as the "queen of fruits." Royal references aside, from a taste standpoint, it is among my favorite flavor "secrets" to give juice that spark of special something.

Benefits The health benefits of mangosteen are still under study, which makes this tropical fruit a bit of a superfood underdog, scientifically speaking. Yet the value of its nutritional contents, which include special phytochemical compounds known as xanthones (which are renowned for their anti-inflammatory, anti-bacterial, and anti-cancer effects), is undeniable. Combined with its special flavor, these healing attributes make mangosteen an extremely desirable superfood to include in juices.

Prep notes Mangosteen is most often sold in North America as a prepressed juice, which I recommend for the recipes in this book. But if you can find *fresh* mangosteen, it is such a treat!

Noni

Oh, noni. Whatever are we to do with you? You're genuinely packed with benefits, and yet you taste so . . . so terrible. Sometimes called "starvation fruit," it remains unclear to me whether noni earned this moniker because of its impressive life-sustaining nutrition, or simply because you'd have to be starving before you'd consider eating such a pungent, bitter piece of produce. Native to Southeast Asia, this light-colored oval fruit is quite popular in health circles, though it rarely appears in culinary crowds.

Benefits Nose-wrinkling aside, noni genuinely is a superfood that offers a truly vast spectrum of benefits. Its antioxidants and phytochemicals reportedly enhance the immune system, decrease inflammation, act as a digestive aid, slow or prevent oxidation, offer pain relief, and even promote a good mood by increasing serotonin levels.

Prep notes For juice recipes, the easiest way to incorporate noni is to use small amounts of pure, prepressed noni juice, which can be purchased from quality sources (see page 203). If by chance you find fresh noni, its flavor will not be as potent as prepressed juice. Since noni juice overpowers other flavors so intensely, I've used it—and masked its flavor completely—in only one recipe in this book, which is remarkably good (see page 161). While I encourage you to use noni for health reasons in whatever form you can find it, I can't help bidding you to take caution as you embark on the culinary uses of this unique fruit.

Pomegranate

Perhaps the only thing more special than the ruby-like juicy seeds found inside of a globe-like pomegranate fruit is the beautiful deep red juice made from pressing them. Sweet, tart, and mildly astringent, pomegranate juice tastes as potently wonderful as it looks!

Benefits The healing potential of pomegranate juice is well established in the health and medical community. Because of pomegranate's exceptional antioxidant content, studies have shown that regular consumption of pomegranate juice helps combat heart disease and lowers blood pressure and cholesterol. In-vitro testing has even shown that it can inhibit cancer growth.

Prep notes You can always juice fresh pomegranates; simply run the seeds through the juicer like any other fruit. Yet, unless you have access to pomegranate trees, buying the fruit and juicing the seeds can be prohibitively expensive. Not to mention the laborious process of opening up several fruits and carefully removing their individual seeds, all for a single (admittedly spectacular!) glass of fresh juice. For the recipes in this book, I recommend using a prepressed juice, preferably a variety that is 100% pure. You will still garner most of the benefits and flavor of this wildly beneficial juice, and at a fraction of the cost. You can find prepressed pomegranate juice in the refrigerated juice section of most markets.

✳ SUPER-ROOTS

Roots are magnets for minerals. It makes sense: For most plants, roots are the first point of contact to absorb the nutrition in the soil (which contains abundant minerals), and they often retain much of this healthy storage throughout the life of the plant. Many of the finest naturopathic medicines rely heavily on the use of remedial roots, which are often so potent that their nutrients must be carefully extracted and used in very small quantities via tinctures and multi-ingredient formulas. There are some roots, however, that are on the high end of nutritional power, yet can still be enjoyed in everyday cooking. The roots in this section, burdock and maca, are of this "food-friendly" variety, and are incredible additions to the juices in this book.

Burdock

This brown, woody, bitter root (also called *goba*) is a popular vegetable in Japanese cooking. As the root ages, it becomes significantly more fibrous (therefore producing less juice), so it is important to purchase the freshest roots possible. A simple test of gently bending the root can provide a key to its freshness—the stiffer the root, the fresher it is.

Benefits Burdock is often used as an ingredient in Eastern medicine due its immense potential to heal, especially when detoxification is needed. Because it is such a rich source of phenolic compounds (a type of antioxidant), burdock is a powerful blood cleanser that also boasts many immune-boosting benefits, including strong activity as an anti-inflammatory, anti-bacterial, anti-fungal, and anti-tumor root. It also acts as a diuretic, digestive aid, hormone-balancer, and liver purifier, and is often used for conditions of the skin, joints, and glands.

Prep notes Burdock is best used fresh, which can be sourced at some health food stores, Asian food stores, and even the occasional farmers' market. The root is usually sold with its leaves already trimmed. Burdock is quite powerful, both in flavor and function, so only a few inches of the root is needed at a time to take advantage of its benefits. It oxidizes quite quickly after being cut and will turn grayish brown, but this discoloration is no cause for alarm (and can be prevented by adding a little bit of lemon juice).

Maca

Native to the high altitudes of the Peruvian Andes, maca is a radish-like root that has been used in South America for centuries. Using maca in juices demands an understanding of its flavor language. In other words, it is potentially delicious, but also somewhat limited. Maca's malty, earthy, slightly sweet taste works wonderfully with other roots and tubers, but rarely with fruits and vegetables.

Benefits Maca is a member of a very special class of plants known as adaptogens, which are reputed to help the body adapt to its environment and resist the harmful effects of stress. As a member of this exclusive club, maca provides energy through sustainable nourishment, and not through taxing stimulants such as caffeine. Instead, maca works with the adrenal glands to equalize the body by managing stress and balancing hormones. In addition, maca is also a proven aphrodisiac that benefits both men and women.

Prep notes Unless you are in South America, it is highly unlikely that you will come across fresh maca root. Therefore, the recipes in this book utilize a more accessible powdered variety. You can choose between a raw maca powder, which is simply milled from the dried whole root, or a gelatinized powder—a more digestible, concentrated version of maca, that has had the root's starch removed. To avoid clumping, I highly recommend using a blender to fully incorporate maca into juice. Please remember that maca is a very potent superfood, and one that should be incorporated into the diet with respect for its healing power. Most people use between a teaspoon and a tablespoon, once a day, for health maintenance.

✖ SUPER-SEEDS

Though you can't juice a seed, including a few choice seeds in juices helps provide nutrients— fiber and healthy fats, for example—that can't be supplied by juicing regular produce. These "super-seeds," such as the ones described below, are adept at keeping your body's nutritional needs in balance, particularly during a juice cleanse, by offering vital nutrients such as omega fats and complete protein.

Cacao

Cacao = raw chocolate . . . Need I say more? All chocolate originally comes from the large seeds, or "beans," as they are called, of the cacao tree. By itself, as an ingredient, cacao tastes like a bitter, unsweetened form of the darkest, most concentrated chocolate. It is not often used in juices, since most fruit juices, and certainly most vegetable juices, are not chocolate-friendly from a flavor standpoint. However, cacao can still be added to some juices that include plant-based creams, or used in juice-based desserts.

Varieties Cacao is often confused with cocoa powder. Cocoa powder is essentially the roasted, toasted, or otherwise processed form of cacao—a process that lessens the nutrition of the cacao, especially when it comes to antioxidants. Though cacao powder is always a preferred form, pure cocoa powder (without added fillers or sugar) may be substituted with successful results.

Benefits The benefits of cacao are overwhelming, and perhaps it is our species' age-old obsession with all things chocolate that has spurred generations of research delving into the healing powers of cacao. From its impressively high ORAC value ("Oxygen Radical Absorbance Capacity," the measure of antioxidant content), which promotes cardiovascular health and prevents oxidative stress . . . to its exceptional concentration of minerals, such as magnesium and iron; to its special polyphenol compounds (called flavonoids) that research studies have shown enhance positive mood states and increase energy; cacao is an easy superfood to love.

Prep notes Use a high-quality cacao powder in juice recipes, and always use a blender to mix thoroughly.

Chia Seeds

This tiny seed, once essential to some South American cultures as a staple food and now remerging as a promising subject of medical interest, can play a surprisingly big role in the realm of juicing because of its versatility. Although ground chia seed powder (and even flaxseed powder, which has many similar nutritional properties and is indeed a superfood) can be used effectively in juices, whole chia seeds are used in the recipes in this book because they can be added to any kind juice without altering the flavor.

Varieties For juice recipes, use chia in whole-seed form. Brownish-gray is the most common color, though you can also find white chia on the market as well (sometimes sold under copyrighted names); the nutritional and flavor differences between these color varieties are negligible. Chia seed powder (finely ground chia seeds) is not recommended for juicing because it can quickly thicken juices in an undesirable way; it does not have the satisfying texture of whole chia.

Benefits Chia seeds are one of the very best sources of omega-3 fatty acids on the planet—not just in plants, but all foods! Chia also contains protein, is an exceptional source of minerals such as calcium, and is tremendously high in fiber.

Prep notes One of chia's unique qualities is a high concentration of a substance called mucilage, which allows chia seeds to swell up to 8 to 9 times their weight when soaked in liquid. Most people find the mouth feel of chia-thickened drinks pleasurable, as the chia transforms into miniature tapioca-like balls that can be chewed, and slide down the throat so agreeably. The key to achieving this textural perfection is to make sure you do a thorough job of mixing chia seeds into drinks; otherwise the seeds will stick together and form clumps.

Hemp Seeds

Small, nutty-flavored hemp seeds help create milkier juices and can also balance flavors, particularly when juicing roots and some vegetables.

Varieties Hemp seeds and hemp protein powder are both wonderful additions to juices. Note that the edible hemp seeds found in the supermarket are of a different variety than marijuana, and do not contain any detectable THC (the chemical in marijuana that produces a "high").

Benefits Hemp offers a complete source of plant-based protein, essential fatty acids, and many minerals—all in all, a wonderful bodybuilding food for strength, endurance, cardiovascular health, and joint health. Hemp is also among the most alkaline-forming of all nuts and seeds, helping balance the chemistry of the body as an anti-inflammatory food.

Prep notes Always use hulled hemp seeds, and use a blender to turn the small, soft seeds into a creamy element within a juice recipe. (Hemp seeds do not need to be soaked prior to blending.) For an even smoother consistency, you can strain the hemp "milk" through a fine-mesh sieve or cheesecloth. Store hemp seeds in the refrigerator for a longer shelf life.

✳ SUPERFOOD HONORABLE MENTIONS

At some point, most of us put the brakes on the number of exotic foods and superfoods we wish to keep in our cabinets and incorporate into our diets. Nevertheless, I always encourage new culinary excursions—it's part of the great adventure of life (like traveling to a place you haven't been to before). With this spirit of variety in mind, it bears pointing out that there are so many *more* incredible plant-based edibles not used in this book. These ingredients were omitted for a number of compelling reasons: They are more challenging to find than other superfoods, they are rather expensive and inefficient to juice, and they're still being studied for their nutritional benefits. But if you are feeling adventurous, I'd like to offer you a few additional interesting edibles to look for. Whether you discover them as fresh produce on the shelves of a well-stocked health food store or scout them online, consider the list below as fascinating potential new additions to your fresh juice recipes. And yes, each of these is a superfood in its own right!

Aloe vera A large plant in the succulent family with thick, medicinal leaves, aloe is an anti-inflammatory food and offers immune system and digestive support.

Baobab* An African superfood rich in antioxidants, minerals like calcium, and vitamins like vitamin C, that is purported to enhance energy and support healthy skin. Found in powder or juice form in North America, baobab's popular fruity, melonlike flavor makes it a wonderful addition to sweet juices.

Chlorophyll extract Often made from nettles, alfalfa, or mint, highly refined chlorophyll concentrate is easily assimilated, highly pH balancing, and can help build healthy blood. Use it to boost the nutritional effects (and the vibrant color) of green juices. Non-mint varieties have virtually no flavor.

Cupuaçu powder* A relative of cacao, this Amazonian fruit has an unusual creamy consistency and tropical fruit flavor. Cupuaçu is filled with antioxidants, fatty acids, and vitamins that boost the immune system, support metabolism, and increase energy. Look for it in a powdered form to mix into juices.

Elderberries* These aromatic, tart berries are rich in antioxidant compounds, especially anthocyanins. Elderberries are often used for boosting the immune system.

Goldenberries/cape gooseberries/ground cherries* An excellent anti-inflammatory food, thanks to a high level of bioflavonoids, these yellow, globe-like berries offer a sweet-tart flavor with floral and peach undertones, and can be found fresh or sun-dried. Goldenberry powder (available at some natural food stores and online) makes for an exquisite zesty flavor boost when stirred into fruit-based juices.

Kelp powder* Kelp is a type of brown algae often used for thyroid and metabolism support. It is also high in fucoxanthin, an antioxidant that offers protection for the liver and blood cells of the brain, bones, skin, and eyes. Though very little is needed per serving, kelp powder has a strong "sea" flavor and is best used in vegetable juices.

Matcha powder A milled form of green tea leaves, matcha protects cells against oxidative stress (anti-aging). Try adding a little to green juices.

Medicinal mushroom powders (chaga, reishi, shiitake, etc.)* This class of edible, powerful fungi provides intensive immune system support and even anti-cancer benefits.

Mulberries* Sweet berries ranging from white to reddish-purple varieties, mulberries are an excellent source of the anti-aging antioxidant resveratrol. Dried berries offer a more intense flavor than fresh.

Sacha inchi* These large seeds taste similar to peanuts and are exceptionally rich in omega-3 fatty acids, protein, and minerals. Whole sacha inchi seeds or sacha inchi protein powder can be blended into creamy root juices.

Tart cherry juice* Tart cherries have been shown to provide incredible anti-inflammatory benefits, which, studies indicate, may help osteoarthritic conditions. Often found as a shelf-stable juice in many natural food markets, tart cherry juice can be mixed into fresh-pressed homemade blends.

Tocotrienol* A powder made of milled rice bran that is exceptionally high in vitamin E.

Yacon root* Often called the "apple of the earth," this tuber offers sweetness at a very low-calorie and low-sugar cost due to its concentration of FOS (fructooligosaccharides) and is widely used by those with blood sugar disorders. Also stocked with prebiotics, yacon can be used to support healthy digestion. Dried yacon slices can be soaked and/or blended into juices to create a sweet, smoky-apple flavor.

*Not used in any of the recipes in this book; listed only for inspiring further exploration.

FLAVOR BALANCERS

Almost any recipe can benefit from minor ingredient tweaks to help balance flavors, and juices are no exception. The fun thing is, not only do these tweaks—or balancers—give a recipe the extra spark needed to catapult from "pretty good" to utterly alluring, they also bring their own set of benefits, many of which are considered medicinal. You can rely on these natural agents to give your juices a signature style:

Lemons and limes
Ginger root
Turmeric root
Mint leaves or extract
Vanilla extract
Powdered spices (cinnamon, nutmeg, etc.)
Lucuma powder
Hot peppers and chilis (including cayenne powder)
Stevia powder/extract

A QUICK GUIDE TO JUICERS

Unless you are talking to a die-hard juice enthusiast, most people will come out with the same admission: Yes, fresh-pressed juice is delicious, it's clearly a boon to your health, and getting onto the juice bandwagon is a total go . . . except for just one little thing: *Making* juice can be annoying. Alas, I've fully been there too. Of course, the real truth of the matter is that it's the juicing *machines* that can be annoying. Why else would people spend hundreds of dollars on prebottled juice cleanses, when they can replicate the same program at home for half the cost? As a long-time juicer myself, now on my fourth machine, I will fully admit to you that it's true, many juicers are indeed annoying to use. The good news is, they don't have to be! It really all comes down to getting the right type of machine, one that will truly motivate you to activate a juicing lifestyle, easily.

TYPES OF JUICERS

Older juicers are embarrassingly complicated. A billion parts have to be disassembled, cleaned, and reassembled every time a juice is in order. They are a terror to clean. My neighbor has an "artifact" Champion juicer in his garage from the 1970s that looks like a machine gun, weighs as much as a tank, and is as mentally taxing as an intelligence test to put together. No wonder so few people juiced back in the day.

Fortunately, the technology of juicers has improved somewhat, but buying a juicer can still be a little overwhelming. There are not only so many brands to choose from, but each machine is constructed quite differently with unique features, not all of which may be essential or particularly useful to you. The most common question I get about juicing has nothing to do with health benefits or recipes, but is simply "what juicer should I get?"

Outside of shelling out thousands of dollars for a professional commercial juicer like the ones used in your local juice shop, there are two common types of machines that are more than suitable (and far less expensive) for everyday at-home juicing: centrifugal juicers and masticating juicers. As you can see on the next page, they are quite different.

Since both of these juicers have strong selling points, choosing between them may feel like a challenge (can't there just be a juicer that juices *everything* perfectly?). Personally, I've owned both the centrifugal and masticating types. And though I can assure you that while my masticating juicer made some incredible green juices, it sat unused for far too long because I found it such a pain to clean, and at the risk of sounding overly dramatic, it always felt like there was more that I wanted to do with my life other than spend extended periods of time making—and cleaning up—juice.

When I finally acquired and started using a centrifugal juicer instead—a *Breville Juice Fountain Duo*, to be exact—it was a game changer. This machine processes juice unbelievably fast, takes just a minute to clean, and the juice tastes great. I actually get excited to use it and it's an absolutely ideal home machine for anyone who wants to incorporate juicing on a regular basis but is pressed for time (like me). Which leads me to the ultimate, truest secret in determing the best juicer on the market: Buy the one you will ENJOY using the most!

CENTRIFUGAL JUICERS

These machines use a circular disk that spins at high speed to quickly pulverize fresh produce into pulp and juice.

Pros

- Juices quickly
- Less produce prep (fruits and vegetables can be inserted in large chunks)
- Easy to clean
- Less expensive

Cons

- Smaller juice yield (extracted pulp is sometimes still "wet" with juice)
- Shorter shelf life of juice
- Noisier
- Less efficient in juicing leafy green vegetables

Best for Juicing high amounts of watery and/or crisp produce, such as cucumbers, celery, carrots, or apples—essentially all of the "base" ingredients mentioned on pages 8–11.

MASTICATING JUICERS

Masticating means chewing, grinding, or kneading food into a pulp, which is exactly the way these juicers work. By using one or two long gears (depending on the model), produce is "chewed" and squeezed to extract its juice.

Pros

- Higher juice yield (especially enables greater juice extraction from leafy green vegetables)
- Longer shelf life of juice
- Quieter

Cons

- Difficult to clean (more parts)
- Much slower juice extraction
- Usually higher price
- Less efficient in juicing watery fruits and vegetables

Best for Leafy produce, grasses, sprouts, and high-fiber produce, such as kale, parsley, and sometimes fresh wheatgrass.

JUICING GREENS WITH A CENTRIFUGAL JUICER

Although juicing beautiful leafy green super-foods and herbs using a centrifugal juicer is not the most efficient method to extract their juice, this doesn't mean you have to get a second juicer! Instead, try a few of these centrifugal-specific tricks to promote a maximum green juice yield.

- Cluster and tightly pack the greens into a bundle. The juicer is better able to "recognize" a solid mass, as opposed to delicate individual leaves.
- Use a large sturdy leaf (romaine lettuce works great) and wrap the other greens or herbs inside of it, like a burrito.
- If you are able to adjust the speed on your juicer, always switch it to the lowest speed possible when juicing greens.
- Use larger leaves, since they juice better than smaller ones—a good reason to buy bunches of "regular" spinach instead of loose baby spinach leaves, for example.

HELPFUL TOOLS

While a juicer fulfills 99% of tool requirements for juicing, there are a few other tools that are particularly helpful to have on hand when setting up a superfood juice-friendly kitchen. You can also find specific product recommendations and sourcing on page 203.

SHAKER CUP

Using a shaker cup is an effective manual method to incorporate powdered superfood ingredients into fresh-pressed juices. Made out of plastic, glass (even better), or stainless steel, these inexpensive sealable containers often come with a sip-friendly lid that makes them excellent for taking your juices wherever you're going. A further bonus: They're very easy to clean.

BLENDER

When mixing juices with superfood ingredients that are not in powdered form, such as hemp seeds or goji berries, a blender is essential. Don't let this extra step deter you: A quick blend can propel a juice recipe into extraordinary new heights, from both from a taste and a nutritional perspective. For example, blending hemp seeds into a fresh juice can produce a creamier, more flavor-balanced beverage, while at the same time adding protein, minerals, and satiating essential fatty acids like omega-3s. With a blender, you can also incorporate fresh juices into other kinds of recipes, such as the frozen treats beginning on page 160. Any type of blender may be used for the juice recipes in this book. However, generally speaking, high-speed blenders will have a much longer kitchen-life with heavy use than their inexpensive counterparts, making them worth the investment. (I've had my high-speed blender for more than seven years now, consistently use it several times a day for various applications, and it still runs like new.)

MESH STRAINER/CHEESECLOTH

A relatively inexpensive item, a small mesh strainer is nevertheless important to have on hand for a couple reasons. First, it keeps seeds from slipping into juice when you're juicing tart citrus fruit such as lemons and limes. And, second, some juices and juice blends benefit greatly from at least one pass through a strainer, which results in a smoother viscosity that enhances the visceral pleasure of drinking the juice. Never underestimate the power of texture, even if it's "just" juice!

MANUAL CITRUS JUICER

Large citrus fruits can be put directly into the juicer if you're using a centrifugal model, but it's better to juice lemons and limes separately before adding them to other juices, since the pith of these types of citrus fruit is especially bitter. If you need the juice of just one lemon or lime, it's probably easiest to simply squeeze it by hand, but if large quantities of lemony/limey drinks is something you foresee making in your juicing future, a dedicated citrus juicer makes fast work of the job. Though there are many high-end electric models and citrus gadgets available, there's really little need for anything fancy in this department. I personally use a simple manual citrus juicer purchased for just a few dollars.

GOOD KNIVES

Don't make cutting produce harder than it has to be! Investing in a quality chef's knife and, ideally, a paring knife, is money well spent. Prep time will go by much faster and you'll reduce your risk of injury by working with sharp utensils. The best type of knife is the one that feels best in your hand. "Try before you buy" at a culinary store.

SEALABLE GLASS JARS

Whether you're reusing jam jars, glass beverage containers, or inexpensive mason jars, it's handy to have a small collection of glass containers (with their tops!) to store and transport extra juice.

BASIC TECHNIQUES FOR CREATING SUPERFOOD JUICES

The recipes in this book maximize the nutrition of fresh-pressed juices with superfoods, each using one of several techniques to incorporate the most incredible produce found in nature. It goes without saying that not every superfood in the world is suitable for juicing. (Seaweed, anyone? Didn't think so.) The large majority of superfoods, however, can be added to juices using the four kinds of incorporation techniques covered in this book.

1. FRESH-PRESSED

Whenever availability and cost permit, juice fresh. In an ideal world, we would have the option to create homemade juices from fresh

whole superfoods whenever we like. But speaking practically here, while we might be able to get spinach or strawberries in this form, there are many internationally indigenous superfoods that must be carefully dried or otherwise preserved prior to export to protect their nutrition. And since we can't all live in, say, the high altitudes of the Peruvian Andes where maca thrives, or in the Brazilian Amazon where acai berries are harvested, we have to utilize these specialty superfoods in the other forms in which they are available (powders, dried fruit, shelf-stable juice, etc.) and incorporate them through the other techniques listed here. Luckily, a wide and rich assortment of superfoods—leafy greens, herbs, medicinal roots, and local berries—can be sourced fresh to create truly fresh-pressed superfood juice.

2. READY-MADE

Oh, believe me, I do recognize the irony of recommending an occasional packaged juice in a book that promotes fresh-pressed juices. But there are some genuinely good reasons to do so, and many incredible superfoods are simply best used in their juicy form from the get-go. Take sea buckthorn, for example, which, among its immune-boosting and skin-enhancing benefits, offers a puckery-citrus taste with honey undertones. Fresh sea-buckthorn is extremely difficult, if not impossible, to find in most areas of the world (including North America), but you can find it as a perfectly healthy bottled juice

JUICING WITHOUT A JUICER

If you don't own a juicer because you're not ready to buy one or you're unable to borrow one—and you don't want to steal one (kidding of course!)—all is not juiceless: You can use a blender instead. While the blender method is a bit more of a hands-on process, it's certainly not difficult. It goes without saying that if juicing is to become a regular part of your lifestyle, a real juicer is a wise investment down the road.

In place of a juicing machine you will need:

- Blender
- Large bowl
- Nut milk bag (see page 203 for sourcing) or 2 sheets of cheesecloth, large enough to cover the interior of the bowl and roughly an inch of overspill on the sides.

INSTRUCTIONS:

1. Chop or dice your produce well and place it in the blender with the most watery and juicy produce closest to the blades.
2. Try blending. If the blender struggles or your produce is hard, add water, a little at a time, just to get the blender processing all of the produce. Blend until a pulpy smoothie has formed.
3. Cover the inside of a large bowl with a nut milk bag or two layers of cheesecloth, and pour some of the mixture inside of the mesh. Squeeze it by hand to strain the juice over the bowl, until as much juice as possible has been extracted. Discard the dry pulp, and repeat with the remainder of the blended mixture.

(see the Ingredients Resources Guide on page 203 for a recommended source). Just because you are unable to juice a fresh superfood does not mean you have to forego its many benefits. In this book, I sometimes recommend adding small amounts of these "power juices" to fresh-pressed juices to boost the profoundly delicious and energizing results.

Another reason to consider prepackaged superfood juices is cost. While it is possible to make fresh juice out of some of the more accessible superfoods—pomegranates, for example—most consumer-grade juicers are not particularly efficient at extracting the juice from them. I have made fresh-pressed pomegranate juice at home (and believe me, it is otherworldly delicious), but this is a very expensive route to take, since you will need to buy an enormous quantity of fruit to make a single portion. If you have the means and the desire to make a fresh-pressed version of any of the prepackaged juice recommendations in this book, please don't let me stop you! Fresh is always best, but prepackaged will more than get the job done too. It's cost effective, fast, and most importantly, it offers spectacular benefits.

3. SOAKING

Another way to incorporate superfoods in your juicing routine is to use them in dried form. Sundried fruit like goji berries and certain seeds like chia take only 10 to 20 minutes to soften and bulk up in juice and can be enjoyed as a delicious textural element or whizzed in a blender to make a smooth concoction. True, when whole foods are incorporated in this manner there is no actual "juice" (which is why they are always part of a fresh juice base), but here's the payoff: No nutrients are lost from these precious ingredients!

4. BLENDING POWDERS

It's very exciting to see so many superfood powders on the market, since they are an ideal way to incorporate many of the more exotic and difficult-to-find superfoods into juice. For some ingredients, such as spirulina, a powder is the only form it is readily sold in. Other times, powders are simply one of the available options. Goji berries, for example, are most commonly found in a sun-dried form or as a juice, but they can also be found as a powder, which can be whisked or blended instantly into

fresh juice without using the soaking method (see the Ingredients Resources Guide, on page 203, for various goji sources). The recipes in this book include only accessible superfood powders that can be found in most health food stores or online, but there is certainly a plethora of other incredible powders (goldenberry powder or reishi mushroom powder, for example) out there. I encourage you to hunt them down, if you desire to, and enjoy experimenting with them! Blending in healthy protein powders is another wonderful way to turn a fresh juice into an energizing meal.

Note: Because juicing recipes are incredibly flexible, you can always substitute one form or method for another, such as stirring in ready-

made bottled goji juice instead of blending in dried goji berries. It may take a little tweaking to get the flavor or concentration right when you make these changes, but the overall healthy effects will be similar.

SAVING & STORING SUPERFOOD JUICES

The process of juicing breaks down produce much like the first stage of digestion (which is why juice is an excellent source of easily-assimilated nutrition). But since it is broken down, it is also more prone to faster rate of oxidation. A whole cucumber, for example, will stay fresh significantly longer than its corresponding juice. Therefore, it is without question that fresh-pressed juices are best consumed *fresh*, from both a nutrition and flavor standpoint: **ideally, homemade juices are consumed within a 24-hour period from time of pressing.**

To maintain optimum freshness, always re-frigerate juices when not in use, and store in a sealed container (preferably made out of glass). Most recipes will last an additional day or two longer if kept refrigerated, with minor flavor fluc-tuation and moderate nutrient loss. Green juices are usually the first to decline, fruit juices follow soon after, and root-based juices can often last an extra day. Vitamin C is a widely used natural food preservative (often listed as ascorbic acid on packaged juices), and simply adding a little vitamin C-rich fresh lemon or lime juice is an ideal way to help retard oxidation.

If you have more fresh juice than you can drink in a timely manner (may this be your worst problem in life), there are several ways to put the excess to use:

Make juice ice cubes Fill an ice cube tray (preferably one that has a cover) with the excess juice, and freeze. The resulting "juice cubes" can be used as nutritional boost in smoothies, or can be dropped into flavor-complementary fresh juices or cocktails for an impressive presentation.

Create frozen desserts The flavor concentration in juice makes it a wonderful base for popsicles, granitas, and even ice creams. See the frozen juice recipes beginning on page 160 for inspiration, and create your own unique desserts!

Think outside of the glass Fresh juice can be used in many different recipes to enhance flavor and nutrition. Fruit juices can be added to oatmeal or even baked recipes in place of other liquids to help naturally sweeten. Incorporate fresh green juices into smoothies, protein shakes, and even cocktails. Vegetable juices often make incredible additions to soups and stews. Needless to say, there are many options to using fresh juice creatively.

SUPERFOOD FUNCTIONAL CLEANSES

Determine your cleansing goals, then take a look at the cleanses offered in this section and find one that is best suited for your needs. Then look for the icons that accompany each of the recipes in this book to structure your personal menu. While every recipe in Superfood Juices is assigned to specific cleanses based on ingredients, you can always incorporate other types of juice recipes into your cleanse.

FUNCTIONAL CLEANSES

SUSTAINABLE CLEANSING

By no means do you need to follow a cleanse program to use the recipes in this book, nor do you need to go on a full-blown cleanse to enjoy the incredible health benefits of juicing. In fact, if anything, I encourage you to take a more casual approach to juicing, and view it as a *daily boost* of nutritious, easy to digest, premium energy. Nevertheless, sometimes taking a more rigorous, fast-track approach to health is desired, and even needed, which is where a bona fide cleanse comes into focus. The cleanse programs outlined in this section can be of help.

"Oh, I would love to join you for dinner but I *can't*. I'm on a cleanse right now," your friend says to you. While feigning supportive enthusiasm, you try to mask a furrowed brow. "Weren't you just on a cleanse a couple weeks ago?" you think to yourself, while simultaneously nodding and mouthing a drawn-out "Ohhh." Many of us have that friend, someone who *always* seems to be on a cleanse. Is this frequency really necessary? And more importantly, is it even healthy?

For some people, "cleansing" is just another way of saying "dieting." And though juices cleanses are undeniably filled with benefits, some can be taken too far. So for clarity's sake, let's take a realistic approach and look at what cleanses truly are, as well as what they can, and cannot, do.

The aim of most cleanses is to flush the body of toxins, provide a bit of a "break" for the digestive system, and offer an opportunity for renewed health through saturated micronutrient nutrition. Specifically, a juice cleanse usually implies a break from normal "everyday" eating, and instead consuming mostly (and sometimes nothing more than) juice for a specified time range, usually a few days. Recently, however, the term "cleanse" has been used on such a broad scale, its definition has become increasingly nebulous. While many cleanses are a genuine source of healthy rejuvenation, others are far too dramatic, ranging from the ridiculously rigid (lacking proper health justification) to the downright dangerous. Being "flushed of toxins" does not necessarily mean foregoing your body's requirements for a healthy balance of important macronutrients including protein, fat, and carbohydrates. And while there is little risk in changing up the dietary ratio of these nutrients from time to time, exceedingly long, drawn-out periods of macronutrient restriction usually lead to health problems. Juices are wonderful, and juice cleanses can be very recharging from time to time, but consuming nothing more than the nutrient-dense liquid carbohydrates in juices alone for extended time frames creates biological stress, a condition that ultimately undermines your best intentions.

Many hyper-strict long-term juice cleanses, with their extreme macronutrient limitations, are hard to maintain. This results in a yo-yo cleanse effect (similar to yo-yo dieting) in people who are "serial cleansers"—that is, making a jerky progression from restrictive cleansing, to binging, to feeling guilty, to going back to cleansing, to binging, and so on. Keeping this in mind, both the juices in this book and the cleanses outlined below aim to promote a more sustainable approach—a moderate, gentler detoxification and rejuvenation that, while effective, will have less of an impact on day-to-day life and won't send you into a whirlwind of cravings.

It's important to remember that nutrients themselves are not the problem: Fat is vital. Protein is vital. Fiber is vital. What you have to watch out for are the not-so-vital (and definitely nutrient-void) forms of foods and snacks that sometimes sneak into our kitchen cabinets and desk drawers. If you envision a cleanse as a *dietary reboot*—a renewed dedication to fueling your body and meeting your energy needs with absolutely nothing but nutrient-dense foods—there is no quicker way to get a jump-start than juicing.

Before you begin a cleanse, it's helpful to determine what, specifically, you are looking to get out of it. "Going on a cleanse" has such attractive implications that it's easy to jump on board, hoping it will be the secret fix to your problems, whatever they may be—clear up skin issues, get over a cold, lose weight, restore gray hair back to color, and perhaps even become a better, more conscious person. The truth is, while a cleanse *can* do some of these things, it is not a magic bullet. I recommend staying away from cleanse programs that make sweeping claims and inflate expectations. Instead, focus on a cleansing strategy that is motivated by a specific purpose, and don't be afraid to tweak the program design or recipes according to your own unique needs.

In *Superfood Juices*, it is this adaptive approach that is behind a recipe structure I call *functional cleansing*. The implications are two-fold. First, as the name suggests, functional cleansing is designed around addressing a specific function; it has a pre-determined health purpose that applies directly to your individual needs. Say you are an active individual who eats a clean, plant-based diet most of the time, and you decide to go on the infamous "Master Cleanse," because, well, so many people seem to be doing it! Otherwise known as the "Lemonade Diet," the Master Cleanse involves drinking a mixture of lemon juice, cayenne pepper, maple syrup, and water throughout the day. If you were to tell me that you were thinking of going on this cleanse, I would challenge you to explain what, exactly, you hope to cleanse yourself of, and, moreover, how this low-nutrient, lymphatic-flushing cleanse would be of much service to your lifestyle. What is your real objective? It's important to push past the blind belief in "cleanses" in general, and get back to basic nutrition first: What can the foods we eat/juice actually offer us, and how can we use them to effectively reach our goals? Once you've determined these factors, use one of the functional cleanses outlined in the next few pages as a guide, then incorporate the corresponding recipes in this book (marked by icons) to create a custom cleanse that's perfectly tailored for you.

Please note that these cleanses are not diet plans. There are no prescribed quantities, for example, and no formal structure. Prescribing these kinds of regimens would imply that we all need the same thing—that a 28-year-old yoga teacher would have the same needs as a sedentary 65-year-old suffering from osteoarthritis. There is nothing to fear, however, in a flexible, more personalized cleanse. Juice is so hydrating, and its nutrition (especially with the inclusion of superfoods) is so immense, that most people naturally find their own level of satiety, simply through the litmus test of what feels good. It's quite difficult to "overjuice," and if you do, your body will quickly give you signals that it has had enough. The answers are right inside of you! Communicating with your own body is much more valuable than anything an expert or a book can tell you.

disrupt everyday routines surrounding food, from lunchtime meetings to food-oriented social events. For this reason, I suggest actually including a bit of solid food while cleansing, to help reduce hunger and maintain an overall feeling of satiety and improve energy levels. Light eating also helps avoid backsliding after the cleanse is over, because the transition to eating solid food won't be as extreme. The trick, of course, is to carefully select the foods you consume. I recommend eating plant-based and preferably superfood-infused foods as the solid elements of the cleanse. Smaller portions and simple foods—such as an apple, or a cup of quinoa with avocado—are best.

A gradual transition to eating fully solid foods is also important. When I was 23, I went on a week-long juice cleanse/Master Cleanse (a hybrid of sorts). My reason for going on this detox

CAN I EAT WHILE ON A JUICE CLEANSE?

Certainly, this a subject that is not without controversy. On one hand, giving your body a brief break from digesting solid foods is part of the magic of cleansing. Digestion costs us an immense amount of energy: About 10% of our daily energy is spent breaking down and assimilating food. Because juice is already a liquid, much of the body's "work" is already done, and that energy can be utilized elsewhere. On the other hand, cleansing can be rather difficult and

program was simple: I had moved to Portland, Oregon, a few months earlier and had quickly gotten a little too enthusiastic about the wealth of breweries there. I wanted a clean start. I had a solid week of mostly successful cleansing, but because I was consuming 100% liquids, my foodie-tendencies were doing a number on my psyche. The minute my cleanse was over, I went out to celebrate at a Mexican restaurant and ordered (vegan) nachos. What. A. Mistake. Within several minutes of finishing my plate, I felt foggy, then dizzy. My face turned pale, and I left immediately to get some lying-down-on-the-couch-action as quickly as possible. My stomach felt like someone was stabbing it, and for the rest of the evening my body felt like it was made of lead. Even though I had only been on a cleanse for a week, eating the nachos was such a drastic change from the juices that it was a complete shock to my system. Lesson learned? Stick with clean foods—light, mostly raw, plant-based meals that are low in fat—for a few days after a cleanse, and enjoy an easy transition back to everyday eating.

COMPLEMENTARY FOODS FOR JUICE CLEANSES

There are two golden rules to eating on a cleanse: 1) Less is more, and 2) Simple, natural foods are best. Try incorporating some of these cleanse-friendly foods into your juice program as needed:

Salads Salads are basically just a way of eating your juice instead of drinking it. For optimal cleansing, create your salads primarily out leafy greens and/or sprouts, with less emphasis on other vegetables. Consider including fermented vegetables like kimchi (a traditional Korean fermented slaw), which can aid digestion. If a more filling salad is desired, use produce such as avocados, which contain healthy fats, and toss in a handful of superfood seeds like hemp and chia for extra protein. Keep dressings simple and clean, preferably using a homemade mixture of healthy oils or nut/seed butters, vinegar or lemon juice, and sea salt or miso paste.

Vegetable Soups Whether they're warm and creamy, or raw and cool, soups are particularly comforting on a juice cleanse because they feel richer and more satisfying than a beverage. Fresh juices like carrot, celery, or spinach can be blended with avocado and a little sea salt for a highly clean, fully raw, satisfying meal. Or for a more warming bowl, try a savory miso soup, blended cooked squash soup, or a brothy vegetable soup.

Fresh Fruit and Vegetables While it's best to juice as much produce as possible while on a cleanse, there's absolutely nothing wrong with having an apple or some jicama slices, for example, if you need to chew something. A little bit of extra fiber is not going to have a major effect on your cleansing efforts.

Seaweeds Nori, dulse, kelp, and other seaweeds are profoundly mineralizing, and may offer some detoxifying benefits as well. Their salty, deep umami (savory) flavor is a welcome balance to cooling juices. Enjoy them snipped into vegetables soups and mixed into salads. You can even nibble on them for a potent snack.

Nuts and Seeds While fats and protein are usually limited while on a juice cleanse, that doesn't mean they have to be excluded entirely. Small amounts of almonds and walnuts, and superfood seeds like hemp, flax, and chia, can go a long way to extended satiety, while providing premium macro- and micronutrients. Read more about the benefits of hemp and chia on pages 26–27.

Fermented Drinks Kombucha, keifer, kvass, and other fermented nonalcoholic drinks are welcome additions to straight juices, and can further propel digestion of nutrients. You can buy fermented drinks such as these at many health food stores, or try one of the juice-spritzer recipes beginning on page 182.

Juice-Based Desserts Light, sweet, and made out of all things good, try any of the desserts in this book, such as the granitas or popsicles.

Raw Chocolate Surprise! A tiny bit of decadence goes a long way on a juice cleanse. Incorporating a bit of raw chocolate into a cleanse is by no means necessary; however, a small bite-sized treat at the end of a long day is a gratifying reward (and one that's also bursting with antioxidants and minerals, thanks to superfood superstar cacao). If you're using store-bought raw chocolate, choose ones made with pure cacao (not cocoa, which has been roasted) whenever possible, and compare nutrition labels to find the one with the least amount of sugar. Remember, raw chocolate is a small treat only, and not a juice-cleanse foundational food!

FOODS TO AVOID WHILE CLEANSING

When you're embarking on a serious juice cleanse—one that consists primarily of juice and little solid food—what you *don't* consume is just as important as what you *do* consume. While not every food on this list has to be a black sheep forever, these items are disruptive to detoxification, and hence should be avoided during a cleanse to maximize your efforts:

- Refined sugar
- Candy
- Additives like food coloring, gums, unnatural preservatives
- Meat of all kinds, including fish and seafood
- Dairy and all dairy products
- Eggs
- Soy
- Grains, especially ones containing gluten (pseudo grains/cereals, such as quinoa, brown rice, or buckwheat, are okay)
- Legumes
- Heavy amounts of oil
- Processed foods, anything from chips to non-whole-food nutrition bars
- "Complicated" recipes that contain a large number of ingredients for one dish
- Alcohol
- Soda

BONUS BENEFITS

Every juice offers a vast array of merits, and, great taste aside, it's often these health advantages that make juices so wonderfully (and instinctually) "addictive." In addition to the benefits outlined in the cleanses on pages 46–50, below you will find an at-a-glance guide to some of the biggest pro's of drinking superfood juices.

QUICK REBOOT Juice provides natural energy, and is abundant in a broad spectrum of vitamins, minerals, and antioxidants.

DETOX & FLUSH Juice is particularly helpful in flushing the body of toxins, raising alkalinity (balancing pH levels), and improving the immune system.

SLIM & TONE Juice includes superfoods particularly helpful in facilitating weight loss and healthy metabolism, and is lower in sugar and calories.

STRENGTH & STAMINA Juice contains nutrients that support an active lifestyle, including plant-based protein and healthy fats, as well as varieties of antioxidants that promote cardiovascular health and act as anti-inflammatory agents.

BEAUTY & ANTI-AGING Juice contains ingredients that boast notable quantities of "beauty nutrients," such as vitamin C (essential for the synthesis of collagen and an anti-inflammatory), healthy fats, and antioxidants for skin protection.

QUICK REBOOT CLEANSE
promotes energy and rejuvenation

Best for Anyone who is new to cleansing, or who desires a gentle cleanse.

Description "Reboot" juices are hugely diverse, ranging from fruit, vegetable, and green juices to many others. For a full day cleanse, choose 4–7 juice recipes marked with a "Quick Reboot" icon, or use the Sample Daily Menu below. *Recommended duration of cleanse: 1–3 days.*

Featured Superfoods Almost any superfood may be used. Especially helpful are well-balanced chia seeds, heart-healthy hemp seeds, and gently cleansing leafy green vegetables.

SAMPLE DAILY MENU
Drink 12–16 ounces of each juice throughout the day as desired.
Foods on pages 43–44 may also be eaten during this cleanse.

CITRUS APPLE 73

CUCUMBER MINT 114

VEGGIE CLASSIC 119

CRANBERRY-ORANGE CHIA FRESCA 175

SPINACH HEMP 122

CACAO PEAR 85

DETOX & FLUSH CLEANSE

*promotes immune system strength, cellular detoxification,
liver and kidney support, and alkalization (pH balance)*

Best for Experienced cleansers, or those looking for a more aggressive cleanse.

Description These detoxifying juices make use of deeply cleansing ingredients, often in the form of green and low-sugar juices. For a full day cleanse, choose 5–7 juice recipes marked with a "Detox & Flush" icon, or use the Sample Daily Menu below. *Recommended duration of cleanse: 1–5 days.*

Featured Superfoods Includes sea algae (chlorella and spirulina), green vegetables, lemon, aloe, camu berry, hot peppers, ginger, and turmeric.

SAMPLE DAILY MENU

Drink 12–16 ounces of each juice throughout the day as desired.
Foods on pages 43–44 may also be eaten during this cleanse.

CITRUS ALOE 78

CUCUMBER MINT 114

LIME GREENS 111

GREEN APPLE KALE CHIA FRESCA 178

CELERY GREENS 101

CASHEW ROOTS 144

SLIM & TONE CLEANSE

promotes weight loss, fat reduction, cellulite minimization, and skin firming

Best for New or experienced cleansers looking to optimize the body's form.

Description Experience the slimming and toning effects of this special selection of lower-calorie and lower-sugar juices. For a full day cleanse, choose 5–7 juice recipes marked with a "Slim & Tone" icon, or use the Sample Daily Menu below. *Recommended duration of cleanse: 1–5 days.*

Featured Superfoods Includes documented slimming foods such as algae (chlorella and spirulina), grapefruit, lemon, cayenne, acai berry, chia seeds, and more.

SAMPLE DAILY MENU

Drink 12–16 ounces of each juice throughout the day as desired.
Foods on pages 43–44 may also be eaten during this cleanse.

GREEN TEA GOJI INFUSION   187

GRAPEFRUIT FENNEL   60

GINGER GREENS   99

ELECTROLYTE CHIA LEMONADE   176

SPECTRUM JUICE   147

COCONUT SPIRULINA   123

Optional: CANTALOUPE SEA BUCKTHORN ICE   166
serving size 8 ounces

STRENGTH & STAMINA CLEANSE
promotes energy, detoxification, adrenal balance, and injury repair

Best for New or experienced cleansers, particularly those who require a high level of energy throughout the course of the cleanse. Especially good for athletes and other active individuals.

Description The juices in this type of cleanse are more "hearty" than most and incorporate roots, tubers, fruit and vegetable medleys, and even seed blends to ensure sustained energy. For a full day cleanse, choose 6–8 juice recipes marked with a "Strength & Stamina" icon, or use the Sample Daily Menu below. *Recommended duration of cleanse: 1–3 days.*

Featured Superfoods Renewing superfoods that offer energy and oxygenate the blood, such as leafy greens, are emphasized, as well as repairing superfoods such as maca, hemp seeds, chia seeds, acai, maqui, camu, and cacao. A few recipes with plant-based protein powders are also included.

SAMPLE DAILY MENU

Drink 12–16 ounces of each juice throughout the day as desired.
Foods on pages 43–44 may also be eaten during this cleanse.

SPIRULINA WATERMELON 75

SWEET POTATO PROTEIN 139

LIME GREENS 111

ELECTROLYTE CHIA LEMONADE 176

CARROT MACA 134

ALMOND CELERY 115

VOLCANO HOT CHOCOLATE 154

serving size 12 ounces

BEAUTY & ANTI-AGING CLEANSE
promotes skin clarity, eye brightness, and hair luster;
combats and prevents the signs of aging

Best for New or experienced cleansers looking to reap aesthetic rewards.

Description For an outer (and inner!) glow, try any of the juices in this cleanse, which range from flavorful berry blends to refreshing green vegetable infusions. For a full day cleanse, choose 4–7 juice recipes marked with a "Beauty & Anti-Aging" icon, or use the Sample Daily Menu below. *Recommended duration of cleanse: 1–5 days.*

Featured Superfoods "Beauty Berries" such as sea buckthorn, acai, camu, and maqui are important as well as ones rich in omega-3s like hemp and chia.

SAMPLE DAILY MENU

Drink 12–16 ounces of each juice throughout the day as desired.
Foods on pages 43–44 may also be eaten during this cleanse.

BERRIES & CREAM 91

COOLING KALE 95

LIME GREENS 111

ACAI BERRY CHIA FRESCA 179
use variation with maqui berry

RUSSIAN SEA BUCKTHORN 142

CHOCOLATE MINT 121

THE FOUR STAGES OF CLEANSING—WHAT TO EXPECT

There is an undeniable physiological roller-coaster aspect to undertaking a cleanse, especially ones that last three days or longer. I refer to this process as the "four stages of cleansing." Though the timing of these stages can vary slightly, depending on personal metabolism and one's original state of health, the pattern is always similar. These four stages are *empowerment, doubt, struggle,* and *euphoria.* (During longer cleanses, this cycle can even be repeated several times.)

1 Empowerment Usually, the commitment of starting a cleanse is very empowering. For the first half or full day, there is a sense of well-being and inner strength that comes from the immense level of care and premium nutrition poured into your body. There's a feeling of "this isn't so bad, right?"

2 Doubt It is entirely normal for a bit of hunger to set in by the second day of the cleanse, which often produces doubt that you can stick to the full course of the cleanse. Good to remember is that this initial sensation of hunger has more to do with a feeling of not being "full" after a "meal," rather than a lack of nutrition. For some people, feelings of hunger worsen whenever they miss the usual gratification of chewing—a craving easily alleviated by eating small amounts of solid, cleanse-approved foods (see page 43).

3 Struggle The hardest part of the cleanse— the struggle—comes next. Skepticism that there is a real need for such "drastic" health measures arises, and can provoke a temporary psychological obsession with food, eating, and chewing, while a mental (not physiological) state of hunger takes over. Needless to say, this is the most difficult part of the cleanse, though it is often where the peak detoxification takes place.

4 Euphoria If you can get over the mental hurdles, the reward in the final stage is sweet: a state of mild euphoria. By now, toxins have been released, the digestive system has calmed down, your mental state is more relaxed, and as you begin to coast into your new system of nourishment you feel light, energized, and extremely aware. This completion stage is one of the most talked-about aspects of cleansing, and such a tangible state of renewal is an incredible physical experience.

CLEANSING SUPERFOOD SECRET: CHIA SEEDS

Chia seeds are a dedicated juice cleanser's best friend. The benefits of chia seeds are many, including omega-3 fats, antioxidants, and essential minerals (see page 26 for more information about chia). But chia's big benefit to cleansing, specifically, can be found in a natural compound called mucilage, which is localized in the seeds. Found in all species of plants, mucilage is the substance that allows plants to retain water for survival between rainfalls. Chia seeds are unique in that they contain a tremendous quantity of this mucilage—a quality that causes an unusual effect. When a chia seed comes into contact with liquid, it "bulks up" in size, forming a jelly-like sheath around itself. This quality is of incredible use to someone who is juicing. It means that for a very low calorie cost, you can incorporate greater physical mass into your digestive system (never fear: chia seeds are extremely easy to digest), thereby reducing the effects of hunger and making you feel "full."

But the benefits don't stop there. Chia seeds are also an exceptional source of fiber. This quality, combined with mucilage in the seeds, makes chia a phenomenal companion to juices—especially fruit juices, which are often high in sugar. The fiber and mucilage in chia actually slow down the release of sugar into the bloodstream (making it a great dietary tool for diabetics), and help prevent blood sugar spikes and crashes while maintaining a stable energy level.

Most people find chia's smooth gel texture uniquely pleasant. In fact, chia has been used in beverages in Central America for thousands of years in the form of "chia fresca" drinks, which more recently, have exploded into the beverage aisles of health food stores across North America. But the best news is, not only can you make easy and inexpensive chia beverages at home, but the seeds can be combined with almost any ingredient in the fridge or pantry for a quick boost.

So, if you find that you are struggling with hunger and loss of energy on your juice cleanse, try adding chia seeds to your juice. There are several recipes for chia drinks in this book (see Chia Frescas, beginning on page 174) that yield delicious results, or you can add chia seeds to any juice recipe in this book (or any juice at all, for that matter) and get great results. (Because chia seeds have virtually no flavor and provide texture only, they can be added freely to juices without altering the taste.) In fact, you can even simply add chia to water and experience the tremendously helpful benefits of the humble little seed. For a simple chia and juice recipe, try the base recipe below (you can use more or less chia, to taste).

BASE CHIA FRESCA RECIPE

Ratio 2–4 tablespoons chia seeds: 2 cups juice
Directions Add chia seeds to juice, preferably in a shaker cup or jar with a lid. Shake vigorously. Let chia soak for 10 minutes, then shake once more to break up any clumps. Allow chia to continue to gel for a minimum of 10 minutes longer. Adding chia to juice does not extend or impair the shelf life of a juice.
Remember Chia seeds are enormously high in fiber. This should not pose any health complications. Nevertheless, life's number one rule—moderation—applies even to chia.

PART TWO

THE JUICES

See, taste, feel—this is the experience of drinking juice. Watching the jewel-like reds, bright greens, cheery yellows, and almost fluorescent purples fill each glass is a cathartic practice in and of itself. Tasting the rainbow, from the most popular local fruits to the world's most sought-after super-foods, you'll find flavors come ALIVE in an entirely new, harmonious way in their juiced form. And of course, the clarity and energy that develop post-sip is something few other foods can offer so quickly and effectively. Truly, juicing is a beautiful culinary lifestyle on every level.

BEFORE YOU BEGIN

In many ways, juicing is a *carpe momento* practice. Unlike the precise measurements and specific ingredients used in baking and cooking, the use of fresh produce in juicing depends less on formal recipes, and much more on a wide range of variables that can affect flavor, color, and yield in ways you can't always predict. Part of the beauty of juice recipes is their flexibility. The sweetness of a juice, for example, might have more to do with the kind of apples you use than the number of apples called for in a recipe. If a recipe calls for a small bunch of kale, the outcome won't be negatively impacted if you use a larger bunch; one particular lime might produce more or less juice than another; and there is little point in chopping up a perfect "cup" of pineapple when nature herself varies the flavor ever so slightly from fruit to fruit. Juices also gracefully accommodate substitutions—if the Swiss chard at the market looks ten times more vibrant than the kale, it will not matter one iota if you swap it into the mix.

Each recipe in the following pages gives approximate quantities for good flavor combinations to create an excellent juice. That said, it is more than likely your own juices will need a little tweaking at some point to account for the infinite variations that occur in nature. Just as other kinds of recipes instruct us to "season to taste," you should feel equally empowered to do the same with the juice recipes in this book—have fun with them and drink well!

TIPS TO REMEMBER

Superfoods are included to quickly enhance a juice recipe's health benefits. If a recipe calls for a superfood you don't have, see page 203 for sourcing, or page 199 for substitution ideas. Many recipes will still taste good without superfood ingredients.

QUICK FLAVOR ADJUSTMENTS FOR JUICES

- **For more sweetness**—add apple
  For a more savory flavor—add celery
  For more mellowness—add cucumber
  For more "spike"—add lemon
  For more flavor (to enhance sweet juices)— add stevia
  For more flavor (to enhance savory juices)— add sea salt
  To enhance nutrition—add a superfood!
- With the exception of Warm Juices beginning on page 152, most juice recipes taste best cold. Serve over ice for maximum refreshment.
- Juices taste best within an hour or two of juicing, but can last (when refrigerated) for a couple days. See page 37 for ideas on saving extra juice.
- Use organic produce whenever possible. If you are using non-organic fruits and vegetables (such as cucumbers, sweet potatoes, and melons), peel them before juicing in order to avoid some of the pesticide residue.

USING STEVIA TO "SWEETEN TO TASTE"

In a healthy juicer's kitchen, stevia is an invaluable tool. A naturally-occuring "sweet" compound is extracted and purified from the leaves of this native South American herb and sold in a liquid or powder form in most health markets. Stevia is an incredibly potent sweetener—about 300 times sweeter than sugar—and yet it contains no sugars, no calories, and a glycemic index of zero. Though unsuitable for use in most recipes because of its intensity, stevia is absolutely ideal to use in myriad liquids and beverages. Added to juices, stevia has the unique ability to not only boost sweetness, but to actually enhance flavor. For example, it makes orange juice taste more "orange-y" and can transform bland-tasting strawberries into delicious-tasting "perfect" ones.

To use stevia in juices, think of using it in the same way you use salt: Start by using as little as possible, then taste and work your way up to the level of sweetness you desire. Too much stevia will create an overwhelming sweetness with a bitter, woody aftertaste. If you're new to using stevia, or apprehensive about using it, I highly suggest purchasing a liquid form instead of a powder, as the liquid comes with a little dropper that makes small quantities easy to control (and remember for future use).

A good runner-up if you do not wish to use stevia is xylitol. This sugar-like substance is a sugar alcohol derived from fruits and vegetables, and has just 40% of the calories of cane sugar and an extremely low glycemic index of 7.

Other sweetening staples in the superfood pantry, such as coconut sugar, maple syrup, agave syrup, yacon syrup, etc., may be used at your discretion, but they are not recommended for use in juices simply because it is so much easier and healthier to use stevia or xylitol. Keep your juices at peak flavor *and* peak health potential with the best sweeteners nature has to offer!

FRUIT JUICES

Warning: Drinking fresh fruit juice will forever ruin your experience of store-bought juices (it's the equivalent of comparing a glittery ruby to a plastic red bead). These recipes offer nature's sweetest offerings in a joyous stream of flavor, like Citrus Apple, Acai Grape, and Kumquat Cranberry. Fruit juices are also the perfect canvas to incorporate other superfruits, in all their various forms, like maqui berry powder, mangosteen juice, and fresh strawberries.

 = FEATURED SUPERFOOD INGREDIENT

 QUICK REBOOT   DETOX & FLUSH    SLIM & TONE

 STRENGTH & STAMINA   BEAUTY & ANTI-AGING

STRAWBERRY ORANGE

Simple and vibrant, this lovely vitamin-rich juice begs for a leisurely morning breakfast. You can also easily transfer the juice to a blender, add a banana, and turn it into a light, incredibly fresh smoothie.

MAKES APPROXIMATELY 16 OUNCES

4 navel oranges, peeled

2 cups strawberries

½ lime, juiced

1 tablespoon maqui berry powder

sweetener, to taste

Juice the oranges and strawberries together. Stir in the lime juice and maqui powder. Taste, and add stevia (or desired sweetener), as needed.

GRAPEFRUIT FENNEL

There's a sophistication to this delicate and well-balanced blend, despite its simplicity. You can always juice the green fennel fronds in addition to the bulb, but I've omitted them here to keep the pink color of the juice as vibrant as possible; I like to keep a couple fennel bulbs on hand and use the fronds as a delicate garnish.

MAKES APPROXIMATELY 16 OUNCES

2 pink grapefruit, peeled

1 fennel bulb, green fronds removed

1 tablespoon sea buckthorn berry juice

sweetener, to taste (optional)

Juice the grapefruit and fennel, then stir in the sea buckthorn berry juice. Taste, and add stevia or sweetener of choice if desired.

FEEL-GOOD FACT
The omega-7 essential fatty acids found in sea buckthorn may help with weight management and insulin sensitivities. Clinical studies show that these amazing fats can facilitate weight loss (and help keep it off), and also help the body convert glucose to energy rather than storing it as fat.

CANTALOUPE GINGER

Cantaloupe on its own makes such a mellow juice. A touch of ginger and a little bit of floral mangosteen give it the kick it needs, turning cantaloupe's nonchalance into something suddenly very exciting.

MAKES APPROXIMATELY 16 OUNCES

½ cantaloupe, seeds and peel discarded

1 inch fresh ginger root

3 tablespoons mangosteen juice

Juice the cantaloupe and ginger, then stir in the mangosteen juice.

JUICE BOOST
Transfer the finished juice to a blender and add 2 tablespoons dried goji berries (or 1 tablespoon goji berry powder or juice). Blend well, then pour through a fine-mesh sieve to strain.

ORANGE MANGOSTEEN

This deluxe, creamy, orange drink is reminiscent of the classic Orange Julius.
It is an absolute pleasure to drink, and is packed with energizing superfoods,
like omega-rich hemp seeds and anti-inflammatory mangosteen.

MAKES APPROXIMATELY 16 OUNCES

1½ navel oranges, peeled

3 peaches, pitted

2 tablespoons mangosteen juice

1 tablespoon hemp seeds

⅛ teaspoon vanilla extract

Juice the oranges and peaches. Transfer to a blender and add the mangosteen juice, hemp seeds, and vanilla extract. Process until hemp seeds are fully blended.

FEEL-GOOD FACT
Mangosteen's biggest claim to fame is its high content of xanthones, a special antioxidant that has anti-bacterial, anti-fungal, anti-inflammatory, and even anti-cancer properties.

WATERMELON GOJI

Believe it or not, basil actually enhances the natural flavor of watermelon.
You can choose to either blend the soaked and plumped goji berries into
the final drink, or leave them whole as juicy little morsels.

MAKES APPROXIMATELY 16 OUNCES

3 cups seedless watermelon, rind removed

1 handful fresh basil

2 tablespoons goji berries

Juice the watermelon and basil. Add the goji berries, mix well, and let the berries steep for 15 minutes until they're saturated with juice. Juice may be blended to fully incorporate the goji berries, or enjoyed as is, with the plump goji berries adding a lovely textural addition.

JUICE BOOST

Use purple basil instead of the green variety to produce an even more stunning red color in the juice—and take advantage of its heart-healthy anthocyanin antioxidants. Look for purple basil during the warm months at farmers' markets, or grow it at home in your herb pot!

ACAI CHERRY LIMEADE

*Acai and cherry transform a good limeade into a great one, packing it with plentiful
antioxidants and friendly fruit flavor. If you don't have whole cherries to press,
you can swap in ⅓ cup store-bought cherry juice. (It still makes a lovely drink.)*

MAKES APPROXIMATELY 16 OUNCES

1 cup frozen cherries

1 cup red grapes

1 cup water

2 limes, juiced

1 tablespoon acai berry powder

sweetener, to taste

Use the freeze-thaw method on page 20 to juice the cherries.
Juice the grapes and transfer the fresh juice to a blender or shaker
cup. Add the cherry juice, water, lime juice and acai powder, and
blend until well combined. Taste, and sweeten as desired.

JUICE BOOST
Use another power berry in place of (or in addition
to) the acai, like a teaspoon of maqui berry powder
or a tablespoon of aronia berry juice.

STRAWBERRY RHUBARB

If you don't have rhubarb growing in your garden, or if it's out of season, buying frozen rhubarb from the store is an incredibly convenient and inexpensive way to enjoy its clean-tasting tartness. (If you have fresh rhubarb, that's even better!)

Note: Never juice anything other than the thick stem of the rhubarb plant—the leaves are toxic.

MAKES APPROXIMATELY 16 OUNCES

- 2 cups strawberries
- 1 cup frozen rhubarb, thawed
- 2 large sweet apples, cored
- ½ inch fresh ginger root
- 1 tablespoon maqui berry powder
- sweetener, to taste (optional)

Juice the strawberries, rhubarb, apples, and ginger, then whisk in the maqui powder. Taste, and add stevia or sweetener of choice if desired.

FEEL-GOOD FACT
Strawberry and rhubarb are more than just a classic flavor pairing—as a duo, they are a nutritional powerhouse. Packed with antioxidants, strawberries have the potential to help fight high blood pressure and skin cancer, for example, while rhubarb is a great source of vitamin C and vitamin K.

ACAI GRAPE

You would never guess that two cups of cabbage are hidden in this sweet purple drink!

MAKES APPROXIMATELY 18 OUNCES

3 cups red grapes

1 sweet apple, cored

2 celery stalks

2 cups purple cabbage

2 tablespoons acai berry powder

Juice the grapes, apple, celery, and cabbage. Transfer the juice to a shaker cup or blender, add the acai powder, and blend well.

FEEL-GOOD FACT

While the purple variety of cabbage may not technically be considered a true leafy *green* superfood, its impressive merits make it an honorary member. Purple cabbage's combination of anthocyanin antioxidants, exceptional concentration of sulfur compounds, as well as stores of vitamin C and K, make it a wonderful anti-aging superfood that's particularly celebrated for promoting great skin.

POMEGRANATE CUCUMBER

As the dried goji berries steep in this hydrating mixture, they naturally sweeten the juice, and the plumped berries provide a fun texture. You can also leave out the goji berries altogether and enjoy the cucumber and pomegranate juice by itself or with a touch of sweetener.

MAKES APPROXIMATELY 24 OUNCES

1 cucumber

1½ cups unsweetened
    pomegranate juice

3 tablespoons dried goji berries

sweetener, to taste (optional)

Juice the cucumber. Whisk the cucumber juice with the pomegranate juice and goji berries, and let the berries steep for 20–30 minutes, or until they are plump and fully hydrated. Taste, and add stevia or sweetener of choice if desired.

....

FEEL-GOOD FACT

Studies have shown pomegranate juice may prevent breast cancer cells from forming, and can kill cancerous cells while leaving healthy ones alone. Pomegranate has also shown to aid in prostate cancer treatment.

....

SPICY PAPAYA

Turn up your digestive fire with this softly heated blend! Papaya is well known for its stomach-friendly enzymes, and cayenne helps give the metabolism a slight boost. For best results, choose a very soft, ripe papaya to maximize flavor, and add a touch of stevia for a sweet flourish.

MAKES APPROXIMATELY 16 OUNCES

1½ cups papaya flesh, seeds and skin removed

1½ cups strawberries

1½ large navel oranges, peeled

½ lime, juiced

3 tablespoons mangosteen juice

scant ⅛ teaspoon cayenne powder

sweetener, to taste

Juice the papaya, strawberries, and oranges. Transfer to a shaker cup and add the lime juice, mangosteen juice, and cayenne; shake to combine. Taste, and add stevia (or desired sweetener) to maximize flavor.

JUICE BOOST

Add a tablespoon of chia seeds, shake well, and let the juice sit for a minimum of 15 minutes to allow the chia to swell. This will create a thicker, more textural juice with extra fiber—a big boost to good digestion.

CALORIES IN JUICE

When you eat with a focus on nutrient density (for example, when you drink superfood juices), calories really do have a way of falling into balance—mainly because nutrient-dense foods are generally lower in calories, and our bodies are more responsive to—and satiated by—ideal nutrition. However, since juicing is often a part of a cleansing program, the subject of calories is one that comes up frequently. Though they're approximations, you can expect juices to contain the following amount of calories per 8 ounces:

AVERAGE JUICE CALORIE COUNT, PER 8 OZ.

Green Juices 50–80 calories (usually on the lower end of the range)

Vegetable Juices 60–90 calories

Fruit Juices 90–120 calories (usually on the higher end of the range)

REDUCING CALORIES

If you're looking to cut calories in juices, there are a couple tricks you can try that will only somewhat affect the overall flavor. For green and vegetable juices, reducing or omitting all fruits, and replacing them with cucumber or celery, will result in significant calorie reduction (if you want a bit of sweetness, add a touch of stevia). It is especially easy to cut calories—and sugar—from fruit juices, simply by adding water and "extending" the flavor with a little stevia. You will be amazed at how much juice you can replace with water, and still get a full-flavored juice through stevia's sweet power. Start with a 50/50 ratio of juice to water, and add stevia to taste. The "stevia-extension" is a fabulous secret in tricking the taste buds and enjoying "lots" of fruit juice without adding lots of calories!

INCREASING CALORIES

For some people, the calories from juices alone are not enough (if they're trying to stay active or avoid losing weight), especially while on a cleanse. Fruit juices can be blended with superfoods—like hemp seeds and chia seeds, or nut butters, like almond butter or cashew butter—and will become creamier and much more satiating. Vegetable juices that include roots can also usually handle the addition of protein powder, and green juices can even be blended with a little bit of avocado or beneficial oils, such as EFA-rich hemp oil or flax oil. Adding a little protein and fat quickly turns a light juice into a sustaining mini-meal of the most energy-giving kind.

CITRUS APPLE

Apples 'n' oranges, our most everyday fruits, get a superfood boost
to become a naturally stimulating juice experience.

MAKES APPROXIMATELY 18 OUNCES

2 large apples, cored

2 large oranges, peeled

1 inch fresh ginger root

2 tablespoons sea buckthorn
berry juice

Juice the apples, oranges, and ginger, then whisk in the sea buckthorn berry juice.

....

JUICE BOOST
Transfer the juice to a blender or shaker cup and add
¼ teaspoon camu berry powder for extra vitamin C.

....

CHILI PEACH

With major anti-inflammatory power coming from half a dozen ingredients, this juice is more than just a tasty treat; it's a real purpose-driven blend. Be sure to use pure chili powder and not a chili "blend" (which often includes garlic, onion, and other spices that are delicious, yet rather unfriendly matches for fresh fruit juice).

MAKES APPROXIMATELY 24 OUNCES

3 peaches, pitted

2 sweet apples, cored

4 carrots

½-inch fresh turmeric root

½ teaspoon camu berry powder

⅛ teaspoon chili powder

sweetener, to taste (optional)

Juice the peaches, apples, carrots, and turmeric. Transfer to a shaker cup or blender, add the camu berry powder and chili powder, and blend until incorporated. Taste, and add stevia or sweetener of choice if desired.

FEEL-GOOD FACT

Because it's considered a spice, turmeric root is more in the category of a "super-herb" than superfood—yet no one will deny its incredible healing power! Among its many benefits, regular turmeric consumption has shown to reduce Alzheimer's symptoms by up to 30%, thanks to the antioxidant that gives the root its identifiable yellow-orange color, known as curcumin.

SPIRULINA WATERMELON

I fully admit, this juice wins the ugly duckling award—it's definitely not the juice to serve someone you don't know. But don't let its murky color fool you: Deliciousness is in full force here, and it's a great energizing hydrator. I make big batches of this one, since it's one of the few juices that last a couple days refrigerated, and it's easy to drink a lot of it. If your watermelon is not the sweetest, just a tiny bit of stevia can really do wonders to bring out its flavor.

MAKES APPROXIMATELY 1 QUART

6 cups seedless watermelon, rind removed

1 lemon, juiced

½ teaspoon spirulina powder

⅛ teaspoon cayenne powder

sweetener, to taste

Juice the watermelon. Pour the fresh juice into a blender and add the lemon juice, spirulina, and cayenne. Taste, and sweeten with stevia (or sweetener of choice) if desired.

....

FEEL-GOOD FACT
Spirulina is one of the highest whole food sources of GLA (gamma linolenic acid), which is considered a "good" omega-6 fat, and often is used to assist in weight loss to help regulate metabolism and decrease the body's insistence on storing fat.

....

PINEAPPLE MANGOSTEEN

From Asian mangosteen, to sweet pineapple indigenous to South America,
what a delicious blessing it is to introduce one "worldly" tropical delicacy
to another . . . and see how quickly they become flavor friends.

MAKES APPROXIMATELY 16 OUNCES

1 pineapple, peeled

⅓ cup mangosteen juice

⅛ teaspoon vanilla extract

sweetener to taste (optional)

Juice the pineapple, then add the mangosteen juice and vanilla extract and mix well. Taste, and sweeten with stevia (or sweetener of choice) if desired.

> **FEEL-GOOD FACT**
>
> Though the superfood mangosteen has no botanical relation to the popular mango, mangosteen's ORAC score (which measures antioxidants) is ranked 150% higher than mango in terms of antioxidant activity.

CITRUS ALOE

If you have an aloe vera plant, lovely! You can use it in this juice: Fillet one of the succulent leaves by separating the gelatinous interior from the skin, then either run it through your juicer, or incorporate it into a finished juice using a blender. (If you juice the entire leaf without filleting it first, the taste will be profoundly bitter.) No aloe vera plant? No worries. Go with store-bought aloe vera juice, just as it is used in the recipe below.

MAKES APPROXIMATELY 16 OUNCES

2 large navel oranges, peeled

1 grapefruit, peeled

¼ cup mangosteen juice

¼ cup aloe vera juice

1 tablespoon sea buckthorn berry juice

Juice the oranges and grapefruit. Mix in the mangosteen juice, aloe vera juice, and sea buckthorn berry juice.

FEEL-GOOD FACT
Including aloe along with other nutrient-dense ingredients can actually enhance their beneficial effects by increasing the bioavailability of naturally occurring antioxidants.

ACAI GINGER

Mark Twain is famously quoted to have said, "Why not go out on a limb? That is where the fruit is." Well, Mr. Twain, while I heartily agree and appreciate your wit, I'll raise you by 2 roots, a few leafy greens, and one very special superberry that likes to grow on palm trees.

MAKES APPROXIMATELY 16 OUNCES

1 large sweet apple, cored

1 very ripe pear, cored

1 beet, scrubbed and trimmed

3 kale leaves

1 inch fresh ginger root

2 tablespoons acai berry powder

Juice the apple, pear, beet, kale, and ginger. Pour the juice into a blender or shaker cup and add the acai berry powder. Blend well. Though this juice can be consumed immediately, it tastes even better if you let it stand for 5 minutes and allow the acai berry powder to slightly hydrate and make the juice extra creamy.

FEEL-GOOD FACT

Acai contains large amounts of plant sterols, which have been shown to reduce cholesterol. In fact, the American Heart Association recommends plant sterols to help adults with high total or LDL cholesterol, and those diagnosed with cardiovascular disease.

PLUM ARONIA BERRY

I don't know about you, but my taste buds love the sweet and tart flavor game, and here you'll find the perfect balance: orange and apple (sweet) mixed with plum and aronia berry (tart).

MAKES APPROXIMATELY 18 OUNCES

4 plums, pitted

2 oranges, peeled

1 sweet apple, cored

1 tablespoon aronia berry juice

⅛ teaspoon cinnamon powder

sweetener to taste (optional)

Juice the plums, oranges, and apple. Mix in the aronia berry juice and cinnamon powder. Taste, and add a touch of sweetener like stevia, if needed.

FEEL-GOOD FACT
Aronia berries offer about 300% more antioxidants than blueberries (their fellow North American superfood comrades).

SPICED POMEGRANATE

Don't let the deep, forbidding purple color of this juice fool you—the ride
from sweet to tangy to earthy to spicy is really quite fun. Plus, with its potent
range of antioxidants, this combination is an anti-aging rock star.

MAKES APPROXIMATELY 16 OUNCES

2 large sweet apples, cored

1 beet, scrubbed and trimmed

½ inch fresh ginger root

1 cup pomegranate juice

2 teaspoons maqui berry
    powder

⅛ teaspoon cinnamon powder

⅛ teaspoon cayenne powder

Juice the apples, beet, and ginger. Transfer the juice to a blender and add the pomegranate juice, maqui berry powder, cinnamon powder, and cayenne. Blend well, then pour the juice through a fine-mesh sieve before serving.

JUICE BOOST

Add ½ cup fresh or thawed frozen blueberries: Blend the berries in when adding the spices, and strain before serving. This can be used either with, or as a substitute for, the maqui powder.

SUPERBERRY KIWI

Oddly, the kiwi is considered a berry by botanists—a little-known fact, and yet its affinity to other "common" berries is well known, particularly in combination with strawberries—a classic pairing. Here, we take this flavorful combo up a notch by including maqui, resulting in a truly super mix.

MAKES APPROXIMATELY 16 OUNCES

- 2 cups strawberries
- 2 kiwis, peeled
- 1 large sweet apple, cored
- 2 teaspoons maqui berry powder
- sweetener, to taste

Juice the strawberries, kiwis, and apple. Whisk in the maqui berry powder, and strain through a fine-mesh sieve if needed. Taste, and sweeten with stevia (or desired sweetener) as needed.

FEEL-GOOD FACT
One of the few green fruits, kiwis contain chlorophyll and are rich in vitamin C and carotenoids.

CACAO PEAR

A juice with chocolate—oh heavens yes! The sweetness of ground cacao in this recipe plays with the freshness of pears like a symphony in your mouth.

MAKES APPROXIMATELY 16 OUNCES

4 extra-ripe pears (such as Bosc), cored

2 teaspoons almond butter

1 teaspoon vanilla extract

2 tablespoons cacao powder

⅛ teaspoon cinnamon powder

Juice the pears. Transfer the fresh juice to a blender, add the remaining ingredients, and blend until smooth.

FEEL-GOOD FACT
When it comes to magnesium, cacao is at the top of the charts, offering more than any other food. Magnesium plays an extremely important role in the body, including aiding in the absorption of calcium, promoting detoxification, and helping ease symptoms of PMS and menopause.

PINEAPPLE ARONIA BERRY

*Like a good dessert wine, this juice has many notes to it
and a taste that lingers long after the last sip.*

MAKES APPROXIMATELY 16 OUNCES

½ pineapple, skin removed

2 sweet apples, cored

1 inch fresh ginger root

1 teaspoon vanilla extract

1 tablespoon aronia berry juice

Juice the pineapple, apples, and ginger. Mix in the vanilla extract and aronia berry juice.

JUICE BOOST

In addition to (or instead of) aronia berry juice, you can use ¼ cup blueberry juice, either store-bought or freshly made, using the freeze-thaw method on page 20.

KUMQUAT CRANBERRY

Kumquats, which can be juiced (and eaten whole, of course) with their skins intact, give this juice an incredibly bright flavor. Mix the juice into some kombucha or sparkling wine and you have an exhilarating cocktail with major "wow" appeal.

MAKES APPROXIMATELY 16 OUNCES

1 cup kumquats

2 large sweet apples, cored

½ cup unsweetened cranberry juice

1 teaspoon maqui berry powder

sweetener, to taste

Juice the kumquats whole with the apples. Add the cranberry juice and maqui berry powder and mix well. Taste, and add stevia (or sweetener of choice) to taste.

FEEL-GOOD FACT
Researchers in Germany have studied the healing connection between cranberries and urinary tract infections since the 1840s. Today, cranberry juice is still regarded as one of the most effective natural methods of promoting kidney and urinary tract health.

GOJI MANGO LIMEADE

Colorful and tropical, this limeade doubles as a nice virgin cocktail.

MAKES APPROXIMATELY 16 OUNCES

½ mango, pit and peel removed

½ orange, peeled

½ lime, juiced

1 cup kombucha

2 tablespoons dried goji berries

sweetener, to taste

Juice the mango and the orange. Whisk in the lime juice, kombucha, and goji berries. Refrigerate for 20–30 minutes, or until goji berries have swelled and are saturated with juice. Add additional lime juice if desired and sweeten with stevia or alternate sweetener to taste.

FEEL-GOOD FACT
Are goji berries the secret to a better quality of life? One double-blind study showed that after just 14 days of consuming goji berry juice (4 ounces a day), test subjects reported higher energy, increased athleticism, better sleep (including ease of awakening), improved concentration, and mental clarity, plus a greater overall sense of wellness and happiness.

BERRIES & CREAM

This violet-colored "milk" is a blissful, liquid luxury of antioxidant goodness matched with beautiful berry sweetness, and it makes a particularly special light dessert.

MAKES APPROXIMATELY 16 OUNCES

2 cups frozen blueberries

1½ cups water

3 tablespoons hemp seeds

1 teaspoon maqui berry powder

¼ teaspoon vanilla extract

⅛ teaspoon cinnamon powder

sweetener, to taste

Use the freeze-thaw method on page 20 to juice the blueberries. Transfer the fresh juice to a blender and add the water, hemp seeds, maqui berry powder, vanilla, and cinnamon. Blend well, and add stevia (or sweetener of choice) to taste. Use a fine-mesh sieve to strain before serving.

JUICE BOOST
Use 1 tablespoon acai powder in addition to (or instead of) the maqui berry powder. You can also use ½ cup store-bought berry juice of any variety, or use 2 cups strawberries and juice them fresh, in place of the frozen blueberries.

GREEN JUICES

Cleansing, purifying, and full of vitality, green juices are arguably the healthiest juices of all. Thanks to the abundance of green superfoods they contain, from leafy greens like spinach, to sprouts like wheatgrass, and algae like spirulina, these juices gently remove toxins from the body while replenishing essential minerals and protective antioxidants. From savory recipes like Almond Celery, to sweet ones like Green Apple Kale, the kingdom of green juices is as broad as it is delicious.

 = FEATURED SUPERFOOD INGREDIENT

 QUICK REBOOT   DETOX & FLUSH   SLIM & TONE

STRENGTH & STAMINA    BEAUTY & ANTI-AGING

GREEN APPLE KALE

For those of you who prefer a mildly sweet green juice, this may just become your new superfood-filled favorite. Ginger and lemon would also make great additions to this blend for an extra hit of flavor.

MAKES APPROXIMATELY 18 OUNCES

2 large green apples, cored

1 cucumber

2 celery stalks

4 large kale leaves

¼ teaspoon spirulina powder

Juice the apples, cucumber, celery, and kale. Transfer the fresh juice to shaker cup or blender, add the spirulina powder, and mix until incorporated.

FEEL-GOOD FACT

Kale contains more calcium per calorie than cow's milk (and it's better absorbed by the body, too).

VARIETIES OF KALE

Few of us would sit down to a tall glass of pure kale juice, but most of us would still agree that kale is king when it comes to leafy green veggies . . . and their corresponding juices. Thanks to its immense popularity, new varieties of kale have started to make an appearance at farmers' markets and grocery stores. These are the most common kale varieties that are best for juicing:

Dinosaur Kale Also known as Latigo Kale or Black Kale, this is the darkest-green of the kales. This variety is characterized by a narrow leaf structure and thin stem. Because it has the highest chlorophyll content and the mildest (least bitter) flavor when consumed raw, it is highly recommended as the go-to kale for use in juice recipes.

Curly Kale The most popular kale on the market, curly kale is chalkboard green and has big, exuberant, curly leaves. It's usually the easiest variety to find, and during growing season the leaves can grow to enormous size. Curly kale juices well, but it can produce a bitter flavor if it used in excess.

Purple Kale This is the newest kind of kale to be carried in stores. With bright purple stems and green leaves that look similar to curly kale, this variety is certainly the prettiest, and it offers the nutritional advantage of anthocyanin antioxidants in addition to a load of chlorophyll. Flavor-wise it can be a little on the peppery side, and should be used delicately in juices.

Russian Kale Perhaps the most forward-flavored kale of all, the flat, fringed leaves of this variety are quite bitter when consumed raw. While Russian kale may be juiced, other varieties such as purple, curly, and dinosaur kale will produce more mild-tasting results.

COOLING KALE

"Chilled-out bliss" best describes the relationship of cooling ingredients in this juice. (Other possible side effects? A case of melodrama. Tucked inside of my original recipe-testing notebook, I described this juice with the wince-worthy, faux-poetic notation: "like I'm taking a dip in a rainforest waterfall on a blistering day." Yeah . . . I'm just going to go ahead and blame the juice on that one.)

MAKES APPROXIMATELY 16 OUNCES

1½ cucumbers

½ honeydew melon, seeded and peeled

1 apple, cored

5 large kale leaves

1 large handful fresh mint

1 lemon, juiced

sweetener, to taste (optional)

Juice the cucumbers, melon, apple, kale, and mint, then whisk in the lemon juice. Taste and touch up with stevia (or sweetener of choice), if desired.

JUICE BOOST

Whisk in ½ teaspoon wheatgrass powder when adding the lemon juice to further enhance the chlorophyll (cleansing) content.

PURSLANE CELERY

In some areas, purslane is a very common weed, like dandelion. Unfortunately, it's not very prominent where I live in Southern California, which means I get disproportionally excited when I can find it at farmers' markets, and have "purslane week" at home, thanks to my resulting purchase. Best served over ice, this juice recipe is one of my favorite ways to use purslane, as it feels both cooling and nurturing, with a bit of creaminess and refreshing sweetness. If you can't find purslane (sigh), you can also use arugula.

MAKES APPROXIMATELY 16 OUNCES

1 handful purslane

1 cucumber

2 celery stalks

2 large sweet apples, cored

Juice the all the ingredients, and whisk together to combine.

....

FEEL-GOOD FACT
Purslane contains the highest level of omega-3
fatty acids of any green plant.

....

GRAPEFRUIT MINT

Watercress, the lovely green featured in this juice, can sometimes be a little hard to handle—its peppery notes can be rather intense in liquid form, so strong ingredients like grapefruit and a good dose of mint are added to this recipe to keep the cress's sharp flavor in check. If you're using a centrifugal juicer, tightly wrap the watercress and mint in a large lettuce leaf before putting it down the juicer chute to extract the most amount of juice from the delicate greens.

MAKES APPROXIMATELY 16 OUNCES

2 large yellow grapefruit, peeled

1 large handful watercress

1 large handful fresh mint

sweetener, to taste

Juice the grapefruit, watercress, and mint. Taste, and add stevia (or desired sweetener) to boost the flavor.

FEEL-GOOD FACT

The proven anti-cancer properties of watercress are huge:
a recent UK study showed that volunteers consuming
just a serving of fresh watercress a day reduced DNA
damage to their blood cells by almost 23%.

GINGER GREENS

Some of us are helpless to resist ginger (greetings, my fellow addicts!), while others prefer to avoid it. Either way, ginger root gives green juices a hit of freshness and spicy intrigue that can take a Plain Jane blend to glamorous happy heights. Ultimately though, you're the master of your own juicer . . . so add more or less ginger to satisfy your personal taste.

MAKES APPROXIMATELY 18 OUNCES

1 cucumber

1 celery stalk

2 green apples, cored

2 large handfuls spinach

½ lemon, juiced

2 inches fresh ginger root

Juice all the ingredients together.

JUICE BOOST
Blend ½ teaspoon camu berry powder into the finished juice to add extra vitamin C.

CELERY GREENS

Although this is a deeply alkalizing beauty of a juice, it is not a recipe for green-juice virgins! It's potent. It's efficient. And for those of you who enjoy a savory, almost broth-like juice, it's perfect.

MAKES APPROXIMATELY 18 OUNCES

10 celery stalks

1 romaine lettuce heart

3 large kale leaves

½ bunch fresh parsley

½ lemon, juiced

Juice the celery, romaine, kale, and parsley, and stir in the lemon juice.

JUICE BOOST

Transfer the finished juice to a blender and add 1 teaspoon almond butter, along with 2 tablespoons hemp seeds. Blend until smooth, and strain if desired.

LEMON CHARD

Of the garden-grown summer produce that remains at the end of a hot season, it's usually lemons and Swiss chard that have a particularly good attitude about putting in the extended growing time. The flavor of chard can vary wildly, depending on the soil it's grown in (mineral-rich soils, for example, impart an especially salty, savory element), so be sure to taste and adjust the quantity of leafy greens you add to this blend. Fresh lemon will help smooth out the green flavor.

MAKES APPROXIMATELY 18 OUNCES

1½ cucumbers

2 celery stalks

3–4 large chard leaves

1 jalapeño pepper, seeds removed

½ lemon, juiced

¼ teaspoon chlorella powder

Juice the cucumbers, celery, chard, and jalapeño. Transfer to a shaker cup, add the lemon juice and chlorella powder, and shake to combine.

FEEL-GOOD FACT
Chlorella (appropriately named) naturally contains the highest concentration of chlorophyll known in the plant kingdom.

FENNEL HERB

A member of the Anise family, licorice-like fennel is a balanced, welcome addition to the fresh flavors in this juice. (Frankly, even the simple combination of fennel and cucumber juice—à la carte—is one of my absolute favorites.) I think you'll find this recipe beautifully invigorating and highly cleansing.

MAKES APPROXIMATELY 18 OUNCES

½ fennel bulb, fronds included

½ cucumber

2 large sweet apples, cored

1 small handful fresh mint

1 small handful fresh parsley

¼ lemon, juiced

sweetener, to taste (optional)

Juice the fennel, cucumber, apples, mint, and parsley, then whisk in the lemon juice. Taste, and add a touch of sweetener like stevia, if needed.

JUICE BOOST

This juice makes a surprisingly palatable base for a lightly flavored or vanilla protein powder blend (plant-based, preferably).

SPICY GREENS

How much spice do you like? In this juice recipe, you can adjust the heat level from mild (by removing all the jalapeño seeds prior to juicing), to ambitiously spicy (if you juice the pepper whole), to anywhere in between. I use this juice if I feel a cold coming on because it is low in sugar and high in immune-boosting nutrients, especially vitamin C and chlorophyll.

MAKES APPROXIMATELY 18 OUNCES

2 cucumbers

4 celery stalks

3 kale leaves

2 romaine lettuce leaves

1 jalapeño pepper, seeds (partially or entirely) removed

½ lime, juiced

¼ teaspoon camu berry powder

Juice the cucumbers, celery, kale, lettuce, and jalapeño pepper. Transfer the juice to a shaker cup or blender, add the lime juice and camu berry powder, and blend until ingredients are fully incorporated.

JUICE BOOST
Add cilantro to this blend for a flavor upgrade, and gain the benefits of its natural anti-bacterial and anti-fungal properties.

SWEET SPINACH

You can really get away with adding substantial amounts of unassuming spinach to this juice without giving it an overwhelmingly "green" taste. The superfoods—leafy greens and camu berry powder—blend into the background like those lovely next door neighbors you rarely see.

MAKES APPROXIMATELY 16 OUNCES

2 cups green grapes

1 cucumber

2 large handfuls spinach

¼ teaspoon camu berry powder

Juice the grapes, cucumber, and spinach. In a shaker cup or blender, mix the juice with the camu berry powder.

JUICE BOOST
For a green drink with more texture, add 2 tablespoons of chia seeds to the juice, and mix together well in a shaker cup. Let it sit for 10 minutes to allow the chia seeds to swell, shake vigorously to separate any seed clumps, then let sit for 10 minutes longer. Will keep for several days, refrigerated.

VANILLA GREENS

*Though it may sound peculiar to pair such a sweet flavoring like vanilla with greens,
the result is a vibrant juice that is as unusual as it is delicious. The addition of a little
effervescent kombucha takes this beverage to the next level of balance and flavor heaven.*

MAKES APPROXIMATELY 16 OUNCES

1 large sweet apple, cored

1 ripe pear, cored

4 large kale leaves

½ cup kombucha (unflavored)

¼ teaspoon wheatgrass powder

¼ teaspoon vanilla extract

Juice the apple, pear, and kale. Pour the juice into a shaker cup, and add the kombucha, wheatgrass powder, and vanilla. Seal the container, and shake a couple of times—just enough to dissolve the wheatgrass powder (do not over shake or you will lose the natural fizziness of the kombucha).

FEEL-GOOD FACT
Kombucha enhances cleansing efforts to eliminate toxins by
promoting healthy liver function and colon efficiency.

PARSNIP PARSLEY

I really don't know what happened. In my excitement at the farmers' market several weeks ago, I suddenly turned into the world's largest parsnip piggy, and ended up with 10 pounds of parsnips in my basket. This translated into a full week of parsnip-based recipes . . . which ultimately included many parsnip-based juices, of course. My adventure was, in fact, a "root awakening" and a blessing (albeit a refrigerator-space-consuming one). Thanks to their assertive flavor and underlying sweetness, using parsnips in a green juice creates a flavor experience that's gorgeously unique to most juices of this genre—an excellent "mix-me-up" green juice.

MAKES APPROXIMATELY 16 OUNCES

4 medium parsnips

2 ripe pears, cored

2 celery stalks

1 large handful fresh parsley

Juice all the ingredients.

JUICE BOOST

Add 1 tablespoon of chia seeds to the juice, transfer to a shaker cup, and shake well. Refrigerate the juice for 10 minutes to allow the chia seeds to slightly swell and form a delectable texture, shake vigorously to separate any seed clumps, then let sit for 10 minutes longer. Shake once more before serving.

FENNEL MINT

Filled with refreshing green ingredients that help the body stay cool, this juice is especially enjoyable in warm weather. Adjust the level of mint to your preference.

MAKES APPROXIMATELY 16 OUNCES

1 large fennel bulb, fronds included

1½ cucumbers

1 large handful fresh mint

¼ teaspoon wheatgrass powder

Juice the fennel and fennel fronds, cucumbers, and mint. Transfer to a shaker cup, add the wheatgrass powder, and shake to combine.

FEEL-GOOD FACT
Mint is more than just a great source of cleansing chlorophyll—it's a bona fide cooling food. The "minty" flavor is due to a natural concentration of menthol, which affects the electrical activity of nerve cells (sensory cells) in our bodies and mimics the sensation of coming into contact with something cold.

LIME GREENS

This is a green juice with a nice savory twist. Often when I'm at home and want a fast, light lunch, I'll make this juice combination, and have it along with a piece of sprouted bread smothered with smashed avocado and little sea salt. Guaranteed mmmph.

MAKES APPROXIMATELY 16 OUNCES

1 cucumber

1 romaine lettuce heart

3 celery stalks

½ lime, juiced

¼ teaspoon wheatgrass powder

Juice the cucumber, lettuce heart, and celery. Transfer to a shaker cup, add the lime juice and wheatgrass powder, and mix well to combine.

SUPERFOOD TIP

Using romaine hearts in juice recipes is a great way to get in more greens without adding "green" flavor. This oft-forgotten superfood is an especially good source of folate, a B vitamin important for energy and regulating mood.

SWEET POTATO KALE

*Sweet and slightly spiced, this could be considered a more "hearty" juice,
and it makes a surprisingly energy-sustaining breakfast or snack.*

MAKES APPROXIMATELY 16 OUNCES

½ pound sweet potatoes,
scrubbed well

2 sweet apples, cored

4 large Latigo kale leaves

1 celery stalk

½ inch fresh ginger root

⅛ teaspoon nutmeg powder

⅛ teaspoon cinnamon powder

Juice the sweet potatoes, apples, kale, celery, and ginger. Transfer
the juice to a shaker cup or blender, add the nutmeg and cinnamon,
and blend well to incorporate the spices.

JUICE BOOST
Blend in a spoonful (to taste) of vanilla protein
powder when adding the spices.

BOK CHOY MUNG BEAN

The first recollection I have of mung bean sprouts is enjoying them as quite a small child, munching on them, unadorned and straight from the bag, entranced with their satisfying crispiness. Mung bean sprouts are one of the most successful sprouts to juice due to their thick and crunchy stems, which practically burst with mineral-rich water. This savory green juice tastes clean and fresh, but could easily be made into a sweet juice by adding green apple.

MAKES APPROXIMATELY 18 OUNCES

- 5 cups mung bean sprouts
- 4 large bok choy leaves
- 1 cucumber
- 1 celery stalk
- ¼ teaspoon wheatgrass powder

Wrap the mung bean sprouts tightly in the bok choy leaves like a burrito, then feed them into the juicer chute. Juice the cucumber and celery as well, then whisk in the wheatgrass powder.

FEEL-GOOD FACT
An organic cucumber consumed with its skin intact has almost twice the antioxidants of a peeled cucumber.

CUCUMBER MINT

Refreshing, refreshing, refreshing. This cooling juice is ever so slightly sweet from the apple and can be enjoyed as is . . . but with a couple drops of stevia, the flavors become even brighter. If you have a special affinity for mint, don't hold back on adding more than the recipe calls for.

MAKES APPROXIMATELY 18 OUNCES

2 cucumbers

1 large bunch fresh mint

1 large sweet apple, cored

½ lemon, juiced

1 teaspoon wheatgrass powder

sweetener, to taste (optional)

Juice the cucumbers, mint, and apple. Transfer to a shaker cup and add the lemon juice and wheatgrass powder and shake to combine. Taste, and add stevia (or desired sweetener) as needed.

JUICE BOOST
Juice a handful of an additional fresh green leafy herbs, such as parsley, cilantro, tarragon, or basil, for additional cleansing and immune-boosting benefits.

ALMOND CELERY

Yum! This bodybuilding drink may appear unusual, but its desirable flavor, along with the wide spectrum of nutrition it supplies (minerals, protein, chlorophyll, and more), have made it a staple in my kitchen. It's a fabulous post-workout juice.

MAKES APPROXIMATELY 16 OUNCES

5 celery stalks

1 large sweet apple, cored

1 large handful spinach

1 tablespoon almond butter

¼ teaspoon chlorella or spirulina powder

Juice the celery, apple, and spinach. Pour the fresh juice into a blender, and add the almond butter and chlorella or spirulina powder. Blend until smooth.

JUICE BOOST
Raise the protein content even further by adding 1 tablespoon hemp protein powder.

JICAMA ROMAINE

Sliced jicama is light on flavor, but high on addictive crunchy satisfaction . . . kind of like a fresh vegetable "potato chip." In fact, the munch-factor is so distracting that the slightly sweet, tremendously refreshing flavor of the jicama really only comes alive in juice form—that's when you can truly appreciate it in full.

MAKES APPROXIMATELY 16 OUNCES

1½ cups jicama, peeled and cubed

6 celery stalks

2 romaine lettuce hearts

½ lime, juiced

Juice the jicama, celery, and lettuce, then stir in the lime juice.

JUICE BOOST

Add 1 teaspoon wheatgrass powder for an extra green boost.

SPINACH PEAR

Spinach is always such a wallflower at the juice flavor party. And while it's quite obvious from its appearance that this juice contains greens, I'd challenge anyone to a blindfold taste test— pear is very clearly the dominant flavor here. The riper the pear, the better the flavor.

MAKES APPROXIMATELY 16 OUNCES

1 ripe pear, cored

1½ cucumbers

1 large handful spinach

sweetener, to taste

Juice the pear, cucumbers, and spinach. Taste, and add stevia (or preferred sweetener) as desired.

JUICE BOOST
Add ¼ teaspoon (or more) spirulina powder to this blend for an extra superfood boost.

VEGGIE CLASSIC

I wouldn't be totally surprised if this simple vegetable combination—which is ubiquitous in juice bars and home kitchens alike—turned out to be the very first juice recipe ever developed. And there's a good reason why it has stuck around: It deliciously "works." Of course, I've added an extra superfood boost to the version here—a little wheatgrass powder that easily blends into the background—to give this classic recipe an extra regenerating punch.

MAKES APPROXIMATELY 16 OUNCES

6 carrots

4 celery stalks

1 large handful spinach

½ teaspoon wheatgrass powder

Juice the carrots, celery, and spinach. Use a shaker cup or blender to mix in the wheatgrass powder.

JUICE BOOST

Other greens may be added to this blend to intensify the cleansing effects. Try a handful of parsley, cilantro, or a couple chard leaves.

CHOCOLATE MINT

Let's just be honest here: This is a profoundly addicting juice, in the very best way. Due to its electrolyte content, it is intensely hydrating and offers a flavor profile that, wonderfully, resembles minty chocolate milk. It is also incredibly invigorating! Anyone who has ever tried it has asked for the recipe.

MAKES APPROXIMATELY 16 OUNCES

- 6 large Latigo kale leaves
- 1 large handful fresh mint
  1½ cups coconut water
- 1 tablespoon cacao powder
  1 teaspoon vanilla extract
  sweetener, to taste

Juice the kale and the mint. Transfer the juice to a blender and add the coconut water, cacao powder, and vanilla—blend well. Taste and sweeten with stevia or preferred sweetener.

JUICE BOOST
If you have liquid chlorophyll, this is an excellent recipe to use it in, which will amplify the green color (and increase the green power).

SPINACH HEMP

*This is the kind of juice that could easily be enjoyed as a light meal. It has
a savory flavor with a slight creaminess that is deeply satisfying.*

MAKES APPROXIMATELY 16 OUNCES

8 celery stalks

2 large handfuls spinach

2 tablespoons hemp seeds

½ lemon, juiced

Juice the celery and spinach. Transfer the juice to a blender and add
the hemp seeds and lemon juice. Blend until smooth and strain, if
desired.

FEEL-GOOD FACT
Just 2 tablespoons of hemp seeds add over
7 grams of easily digestible plant-based protein
and contain all of the essential amino acids.

COCONUT SPIRULINA

You don't even need a juicer to make this extra-fast green juice, and the results are so delicious!
I like the addition of vanilla and stevia, but you can just as easily leave them out.

MAKES APPROXIMATELY 16 OUNCES

2 cups coconut water

1 teaspoon spirulina powder

³⁄₄ teaspoon vanilla extract (optional)

sweetener, to taste (optional)

Use a shaker cup or blender to mix together the coconut water, spirulina powder, and vanilla extract. Add a touch of sweetener like stevia, as desired.

FEEL-GOOD FACT

Coconut water is an exceptionally good source of electrolytes, which break down into electrically charged particles (ions) when dissolved in water. These particles help balance biological chemistry and pH levels, and are used for every electrical interaction in the body . . . . In other words, they affect the function of every cell of your being!

GINGERY APPLE BROCCOLI

Apple has a lovely way of calming broccoli's often, er, "well-announced" flavor . . . and a bit of ginger gives this juice a refreshing heat. If you're looking to hide the flavor of the broccoli entirely, simply juice an additional apple, or add a touch of stevia.

MAKES APPROXIMATELY 16 OUNCES

2 large sweet apples, cored

3 cups chopped broccoli

2 celery stalks

1 inch fresh ginger root

1 lemon, juiced

sweetener, to taste (optional)

Juice the apples, broccoli, celery, and ginger root. Stir in the lemon juice. Add a touch of sweetener like stevia, as desired.

JUICE BOOST
For an extra green boost, add ½ teaspoon spirulina powder (or more, to taste) and mix in a shaker cup or blender to incorporate.

VEGETABLE JUICES

At one time, tomato juice was as far as the subject of "vegetable juice" went (tomatoes are technically a fruit, in any case). Now we know better: Not only is there a whole world of produce out there, waiting to be juiced, but there is no better way to enjoy the tremendous health benefits of large quantities of vegetables than a well-crafted drink. Creamy juices of sweet carrots and tubers often take the base-ingredient position, inviting the use of healing superfoods like maca and sea buckthorn, in addition to protein-rich foods like hemp seeds and even protein powders. From Pumpkin Protein to Cashew Roots, the recipes in this section will make drinking your vegetables something to look forward to.

 = FEATURED SUPERFOOD INGREDIENT

 QUICK REBOOT  DETOX & FLUSH  SLIM & TONE

 STRENGTH & STAMINA   BEAUTY & ANTI-AGING

BURDOCK & ROOTS

Depending on its freshness, a burdock root can sometimes be quite bitter.
Start by juicing half of a root, and add more depending on the flavor.
Extra carrots can also be added for balance if needed.

MAKES APPROXIMATELY 20 OUNCES

½ burdock root (approximately 5–6 inches)

8–10 carrots

1 beet, scrubbed and trimmed

1 apple, cored

1 celery stalk

1 lime, juiced

Juice the burdock, carrots, beet, apple, and celery. Then mix in the lime juice.

FEEL-GOOD FACT

In Chinese medicine, burdock root is used to help treat sore throats and cold symptoms. Thanks to antioxidants like quercetin, burdock root also has strong anti-inflammatory properties that can help with skin conditions (such as eczema) and joint pain (such as arthritis).

SEA BUCKTHORN BEET

*Sit down for this one. Really. This stunning juice is a dreamy flavor medley that makes
your body feel so richly healthy, you'll want to take a moment to bask in it.*

MAKES APPROXIMATELY 18 OUNCES

2 small beets, scrubbed and
trimmed

2 large navel oranges, peeled

3 tablespoons sea buckthorn
berry juice

Juice the beets and the oranges, then whisk in the sea buckthorn
berry juice.

FEEL-GOOD FACT
Thanks to its impressive nitrate content, drinking beet juice
regularly has been shown to help lower blood pressure, increase
cardiovascular function, and even enhance athletic performance.
One famous documentation of beet juice's power involved
Tour de France cyclists, who rode on average a 2.7–2.8%
faster pace after consuming a pint of beet juice pre-race.

CARROT GOJI

Carrots and goji berries, both excellent sources of the eyesight-preserving antioxidant carotene, also taste great together. And, between all the vitamin A and vitamin C they offer, your immune system will be pretty happy too! To my fellow ginger lovers, take note: This blend can easily handle additional ginger root.

MAKES APPROXIMATELY 18 OUNCES

10 carrots

2 celery stalks

1 inch ginger root

2 tablespoons goji berries

Juice the carrots, celery, and ginger root. Transfer the fresh juice to a blender and add the goji berries. Blend very well, then pour the juice through a fine-mesh sieve to strain.

JUICE BOOST
Stir in 1 tablespoon of sea buckthorn berry juice to add additional antioxidant-rich fats.

ACAI YAM

Sweet, creamy, and milky, yam juice is an unexpected delight ... and the perfect base for acai's richness and soft berry undertones. This is an indulgent-feeling juice with nothing but great things to offer, like antioxidants, healthy fats, and sugar-stabilizing spices.

MAKES APPROXIMATELY 16 OUNCES

½ pound yam, well scrubbed

2 carrots

1 cup coconut water, chilled

1 tablespoon acai powder

1 tablespoon almond butter

Juice the yam and carrots. Pour the juice into a blender and add the remaining ingredients. Blend well into a creamy mixture.

JUICE BOOST
Add ½ teaspoon wheatgrass powder as a way to "sneak in" the equivalent of a shot of wheatgrass.

PARSNIP HEMP

Parsnips add a very bold flavor to juices, and this high-wattage sweet recipe is certainly no exception. The creaminess of blended hemp seeds, however, helps bring the spicy exuberance of fresh parsnips back down to earth, and a couple well-placed spices bring it all home. This is a great juice for those who like big flavor.

MAKES APPROXIMATELY 16 OUNCES

4 medium parsnips

2 large sweet apples, cored

1 inch fresh ginger root

¼ cup hemp seeds

1 teaspoon wheatgrass powder

⅛ teaspoon vanilla extract

⅛ teaspoon cinnamon powder

Juice the parsnips, apples, and ginger root. Transfer the fresh juice to a blender, and add the hemp seeds, wheatgrass powder, vanilla extract, and cinnamon. Blend until smooth and creamy.

JUICE BOOST
Add liquid chlorella extract (about 25 drops) to heighten the green color and boost alkalinity.

PUMPKIN PROTEIN

It's a tight race, but I think I'm prepared to call kabocha squash my very favorite winter squash of all. Also called "Japanese pumpkin," it is one of the sweetest and most flavorful of the hard squashes—it really puts a "regular" pumpkin to shame. Juiced here, it offers great pumpkin flavor, and, as an additional bonus, you can juice and consume the nutritious green skin along with the sweet orange flesh. This is an especially good blend to boost with a bit of stevia to bring out the almost pie-like flavors.

MAKES APPROXIMATELY 18 OUNCES

1 pound kabocha squash, seeds removed

1 carrot

1 inch fresh ginger root

1 cup coconut water

1 tablespoon almond butter

2 tablespoons hemp protein powder

¾ teaspoon pumpkin pie spice powder

¼ teaspoon vanilla extract

sweetener, to taste (optional)

Juice the kabocha squash, carrot, and ginger root. Pour into a blender, add the remaining ingredients, and blend well. For a smoother beverage, strain before serving. Add a touch of sweetener, such as stevia, if desired.

JUICE BOOST
Use 1 full serving/scoop of your favorite vanilla protein powder blend in place of the hemp protein powder and vanilla.

CARROT MACA

I think this juice tastes a little bit like a toasted marshmallow.

MAKES APPROXIMATELY 16 OUNCES

16 carrots

1 tablespoon maca powder

2 tablespoons raw cashews

Juice the carrots. Pour the fresh juice into a blender, add the maca and cashews, and blend until smooth. Press through a fine-mesh sieve for a silkier texture.

VARIATION

Blend with a generous amount of ice and a touch of stevia to create a delicious, low-calorie slushie.

MACA YAM

*If you enjoy the flavor of maca, you'll love this creamy drink,
which showcases its slightly buttery undertones.*

MAKES APPROXIMATELY 16 OUNCES

2 pounds yams, well scrubbed

3 tablespoons unsweetened
coconut shreds

2 teaspoons maca powder

scant ¼ teaspoon cinnamon
powder

scant ⅛ teaspoon nutmeg
powder

Juice the yams. Pour the fresh juice into a blender, add the remaining ingredients, and blend until smooth. Press through a fine-mesh sieve if a smoother drink is desired.

FEEL-GOOD FACT

Maca helps balance hormones in both men and women in a natural way, and studies show that it can increase libido by 180%.

CARROT DILL

Faced with an abundance of home-grown herbs that dutifully pop up every spring, I have no choice but to constantly find ways to use them all. (My favorite kind of problem.) This creamy blend is savory and sweet at the same time, with a unique characteristic note of fresh dill.

MAKES APPROXIMATELY 16 OUNCES

5 carrots

1 cucumber

2 celery stalks

⅓ cup fresh dill

4 leaves Swiss chard

2 tablespoons hemp seeds

Juice the carrots, cucumber, and celery. Wrap the dill tightly inside the Swiss chard leaves and juice as well. Transfer the juice to a blender and add the hemp seeds; blend until smooth. Strain if desired.

JUICE BOOST
Add 1 teaspoon wheatgrass powder to the blender to extend the spectrum of vitamins and minerals in this blend.

SWEET POTATO PROTEIN

As soothing as a light cream, sweet potato juice is more like milk than vegetable juice. Combine it with your favorite vanilla-flavored, plant-based protein powder and create a quick shake that's so delicious and energizing, you may just find yourself with a new healthy craving on your hands.

MAKES APPROXIMATELY 16 OUNCES

2 pounds sweet potatoes, well scrubbed

1 serving vanilla protein powder

1 teaspoon wheatgrass powder

⅛ teaspoon nutmeg powder

Juice the sweet potatoes. In a shaker cup or blender, combine the juice with the protein powder, wheatgrass powder, and nutmeg. Blend well, into a creamy mixture.

FEEL-GOOD FACT

When protein powders are made from plants, the advantages are great. These proteins are easy to digest, are hypo-allergenic (with the exception of soy), promote better pH balance, and help speed recovery and cellular repair through their inherent anti-inflammatory qualities. Look for packaged blends that include superfoods like hemp, chia, spirulina/chlorella, and even powdered greens. (See recommendations on page 203.)

LUCUMA CARROT

Sorry plain carrot juice, you've got nothing on this sweet, creamy superfood blend. Fresh lucuma fruit is often described as tasting like a very sweet, sweet potato, which explains why it might greatly enhance a simple run-of-the-mill carrot juice. Since it is rarely available fresh in North America, I use the more accessible lucuma powder to make this a special drink (see page 203 for sourcing lucuma powder).

MAKES APPROXIMATELY 16 OUNCES

10 carrots

1 tablespoon lucuma powder

1 tablespoon hemp seeds

Juice the carrots. Transfer the fresh juice to a blender, and add the lucuma powder and hemp seeds. Blend well, and strain through a fine-mesh sieve if desired.

SUPERFOOD TIP

Lucuma powder is, admittedly, an exotic ingredient that is rarely used in this book. It's a lovely ingredient to consider acquiring, though, because of its unique maple-like sweetness. It is also considered a "smart sweetener," since it enhances flavor and sweetens without adding sugar. Lucuma makes an exhilarating addition to virtually any kind of root juice, and even many fruit juices—especially ones that have an apple, pear, or tropical fruit base; it's definitely a fun ingredient to experiment with. If you choose to add lucuma powder to your pantry, you can also use it in many other types of recipes—from desserts to soups to smoothies—which explains why it makes such a prominent appearance in my other books, *Superfood Kitchen* and *Superfood Smoothies*.

CARROT CAYENNE

Lightly sweet and mildly spicy, this is an essential juice recipe for anyone who loves a little pepper-induced heat.

MAKES APPROXIMATELY 16 OUNCES

5 carrots

1 celery stalk

1 large sweet apple, cored

3 large romaine lettuce leaves

⅛ teaspooon cayenne powder

Juice the carrots, celery, apple, and lettuce, then whisk in the cayenne.

JUICE BOOST
Add ½ teaspoon wheatgrass powder.

RUSSIAN SEA BUCKTHORN

I must give credit where credit is due: This drink is actually a dairy-free, sugar-free version of a very traditional Russian drink that uses sea buckthorn berries. Based on creaminess and flavor alone, it's easy to understand why it's such a classic. A tiny bit of stevia goes a long way to take this smooth beverage to sweet perfection.

MAKES APPROXIMATELY 16 OUNCES

4 carrots

2 tablespoons sea buckthorn berry juice

1 cup coconut water

¼ cup raw cashews

sweetener, to taste

Juice the carrots. Transfer the fresh juice to a blender and add the sea buckthorn berry juice, coconut water, and cashews. Blend until smooth and creamy, and strain if needed. Add a touch of sweetener like stevia, as desired.

JUICE BOOST
Add 1 tablespoon mangosteen juice to gain a broader spectrum of phytonutrients.

CASHEW ROOTS

If you blend in a little raw avocado, this could easily be a light raw soup.
I love how filling it is, even though the ingredients are so light.

MAKES APPROXIMATELY 16 OUNCES

2 carrots

2 medium beets, scrubbed and trimmed

5 celery stalks

¼ cup raw cashews

¼ teaspoon spirulina powder (or more, to taste)

Blend the carrots, beets, and celery. Transfer the juice to a blender, and add the cashews and spirulina. Blend well, then press through a fine-sieve strainer for the smoothest consistency.

JUICE BOOST
Add ½ teaspoon maca powder for a potent (and delicious) rejuvenating boost.

SPICY DAIKON

As the name of this juice suggests, this recipe has a fair bit of heat, thanks to the daikon radish. Start with the smaller amount of daikon, and add more as you see fit.

MAKES APPROXIMATELY 18 OUNCES

6 carrots

¼–½ daikon radish

1 cucumber

1 celery stalk

1 large handful fresh parsley

¼ teaspoon camu berry powder

Juice the carrots, daikon, cucumber, celery, and parsley. Add the camu berry powder and blend using a shaker cup or blender.

JUICE BOOST

Pour the juice into a blender and add 2 tablespoons of dried goji berries. Blend well. Strain if a smoother texture is desired.

SPECTRUM JUICE

This juice gets everything in: roots, fruits, greens from the earth, and greens from the water. It's nice to take a moment to soak in the beauty of these well-balanced and slightly sweet ingredients before you juice them . . . pretty nice to see the bountiful beauty you're giving your body, right?

MAKES APPROXIMATELY 16 OUNCES

5 carrots

1 medium beet, scrubbed and trimmed

1 large sweet apple, cored

5 large kale leaves

1 lime, juiced

¼ teaspoon spirulina powder

Juice the carrots, beet, apple, and kale. Transfer the juice to a shaker cup or blender, and add the lime juice and spirulina, then blend until ingredients are fully incorporated.

JUICE BOOST
Blend in additional spirulina, ¼ teaspoon at a time (to taste), to increase the amount of minerals in the juice.

FENNEL ARONIA BERRY

Sweet and savory at the same time, this potent juice is brimming with antioxidants. You could also swap out the aronia berry juice for other potent purple superfood berries like maqui powder or acai powder.

MAKES APPROXIMATELY 16 OUNCES

1½ ripe pears, cored

1 fennel bulb, green fronds removed

2 celery stalks

½ tablespoon aronia berry juice

¼ teaspoon vanilla extract

Juice the pear, fennel, and celery. Stir in the aronia juice and vanilla extract.

JUICE BOOST

Add ¼ teaspoon camu berry powder for extra vitamin C.

TOMATO CELERY

I hate to tell you this, but drinking that notorious tomato-juice-in-a-can was, unfortunately, a favorite pastime of mine (why hello there, day's worth of salt in a glass). Luckily, this fresh version is a billion times better, both benefit- and taste-wise. With a well-rounded flavor, the tomato is not overly prominent in this recipe, but if you want it more in the foreground, simply increase the tomato-to-carrot ratio.

MAKES APPROXIMATELY 18 OUNCES

4 Roma tomatoes

3 carrots

8 celery stalks

2 tablespoons hemp seeds

2 tablespoons goji berries

pinch cayenne pepper (optional)

pinch sea salt (optional)

FEEL-GOOD FACT
Right alongside coconut water, celery is among the best natural sources of hydrating electrolytes.

Juice the tomatoes, carrots, and celery. Transfer the juice to a blender and add the hemp seeds, goji berries, cayenne pepper, and sea salt. Blend until smooth and creamy.

ARONIA BEET

I challenge you to find a more vibrantly colored juice! What a stunner. And remember, color = antioxidants.

MAKES APPROXIMATELY 16 OUNCES

2 red beets, trimmed and scrubbed

1 cucumber

2 celery stalks

 1 tablespoon aronia berry juice

Juice the beets, cucumber, and celery, then mix in the aronia berry juice.

FEEL-GOOD FACT
There is such a large concentration of anthocyanins in aronia berries that these antioxidants account for 1.5% of the berry's entire weight—a clear reason why aronia berries are linked to helping control oxidative stress (aging).

SEA BUCKTHORN BELL PEPPER

This juice almost has the flavor profile of a light soup. The sea buckthorn brightens the sweet red bell pepper with a touch of acidity.

MAKES APPROXIMATELY 16 OUNCES

2 red bell peppers, seeds and stem removed

2 Roma tomatoes

2 celery stalks

1 tablespoon sea buckthorn berry juice

pinch cayenne pepper

Juice the red bell peppers, tomatoes, and celery. Stir in the sea buckthorn berry juice and cayenne.

JUICE BOOST
To sneak in a little green nutrition, add ½ teaspoon spirulina or wheatgrass powder, or juice a handful of parsley along with the other ingredients.

WARM JUICES

Especially during the colder seasons, a warm juice is a comforting healthy ally. If you have a high-speed blender, you can skip using the stovetop altogether and simply warm the recipe directly in the blender by processing on high for a couple minutes. Beyond the recipes in this section, many of the vegetable juices (beginning on page 126), can be gently warmed up with enormous success as well.

 = FEATURED SUPERFOOD INGREDIENT

 QUICK REBOOT  DETOX & FLUSH  SLIM & TONE

 STRENGTH & STAMINA  BEAUTY & ANTI-AGING

SPICED FRESH CIDER

*Not long after the creation of fresh apple juice came the introduction
of hot apple cider—the epitome of cold weather coziness in a mug.
This fabulously complex-tasting juice warms the body and the spirit.*

MAKES APPROXIMATELY 3 CUPS

2 large sweet apples, cored

2 very ripe pears, cored

1 small fennel bulb, green parts removed

1 inch fresh ginger root

1 teaspoon vanilla extract

½ teaspoon cinnamon powder

2 tablespoons sea buckthorn berry juice

Juice the apples, pears, fennel, and ginger. Transfer the juice to a soup pot, then whisk in the vanilla extract and cinnamon powder. Heat gently over medium heat until hot but not boiling. Stir in the sea buckthorn berry juice just before serving.

VARIATION
Use different spice blends to add flavor complexity, such as cloves, nutmeg, and even black pepper.

VOLCANO HOT CHOCOLATE

This, my friends, is the richest, most divine hot chocolate. I call it "volcano" because its deep red color (from beet juice) reminds me of lava, yet its flavorful explosion is focused on nothing more than creamy chocolate (chocolcano?). Beets sweeten the recipe while also giving a welcome earthy undertone to the raw cacao. As a bit of a dessert drink, this recipe uses a more traditional liquid sweetener in place of stevia or xylitol, which is needed to fully balance out the cacao.

MAKES APPROXIMATELY 3 CUPS

1 cup fresh beet juice (about 2–3 beets, scrubbed and trimmed

½ cup raw cashews

¼ cup cacao powder

2 tablespoons liquid sweetener, such as agave

1½ cups coconut water

Use a blender to process all the ingredients into a smooth cream. Transfer the contents to a soup pot, and gently heat until hot and frothy but not boiling. Serve warm.

FEEL-GOOD FACT

Cacao powder has one of the highest antioxidant scores of any food known: a whopping 95,000 ORAC value per 100 grams. Compare that to apples, which average 5,000 ORAC for the same quantity.

FRESH VEGETABLE BROTH

Most vegetable broths are made from cooked-down vegetables, which slowly infuse their flavors into hot water after hours of simmering. Using fresh juice is a much faster, far more flavorful method, and it preserves infinitely more of the vegetables' micronutrient content. Sipping this warm, savory broth out of a mug is deeply comforting all on its own. Or you can use it as a flavorful base for any recipe where a stock is needed.

MAKES APPROXIMATELY 1 QUART

1 whole bunch celery

4 carrots

½ sweet potato

3 Roma tomatoes

½ leek, white parts only (optional)

2 large handfuls spinach

1 large handful fresh parsley

½ lemon, juiced

Juice all the ingredients except the lemon. Transfer to a soup pot and heat gently until warm, then whisk in the lemon juice.

....

JUICE BOOST

Pour the warm soup into a blender and add ¼ cup hemp seeds to make a creamier soup that's full of essential fatty acids.

....

SPICED ROOTS

Maca's complex flavor adds a veil of sophistication to this festive-tasting blend, which has a froth like a fine latte, and a creamy sweetness that competes with most decadent of comfort drinks. I especially love serving this mix around the holidays.

MAKES APPROXIMATELY 16 OUNCES

5 carrots

1 parsnip

½ pound sweet potatoes, well scrubbed

1 large sweet apple, cored

½ inch fresh ginger root

¼ cup hemp seeds

1 teaspoon maca powder

⅛ teaspoon cinnamon powder

Juice the carrots, parsnip, sweet potatoes, apple, and ginger. Transfer the juice to a blender and add the hemp seeds, maca powder, and cinnamon; blend until smooth. Pour the mixture into a soup pot and gently heat until hot but not boiling. Serve warm.

FEEL-GOOD FACT
Cinnamon, which is, in fact, the bark of a tropical Asian tree, helps balance blood sugar and may even help prevent Alzheimer's, according to recent studies.

LAVENDER ROSE

As a ten-year-old, I was so utterly obsessed with Nancy Drew mystery novels that I wrote my own story, "The Mystery of the Lavender Rose." Spoiler alert: Not only does this similarly titled recipe contain no clues (to the best mystery story EVER written), but the beautiful lavender color comes from the vibrantly colored antioxidants in the maqui berry powder and not *from the flower. The result is a sweet and creamy warm drink with a slightly floral (rose) flavor that looks as enchanting as it tastes. Case closed.*

MAKES APPROXIMATELY 16 OUNCES

4 apples, cored

1½ tablespoons dried rose petals

1 teaspoon maqui berry powder

2 tablespoons hemp seeds

Juice the apples. Pour the fresh juice into a saucepan and bring to a boil. Remove from heat, and steep the rose petals inside for 5 minutes. Mix in the maqui berry powder, strain completely and discard the flowers, then pour the liquid infusion into a blender. Add the hemp seeds, and blend until smooth. Serve warm, re-warming gently on the stovetop only if needed.

SUPERFOOD TIP

Find dried rose petals or miniature roses in the tea section of many stores. Or, if you have access to an organic garden that grows the flowers, dry and use your own.

FROZEN TREATS

Sweet juices are the kick-start to a whole world of creative, healthy dessert recipes, where their natural sweetness helps create full-flavored yet low-sugar delights. While you can freeze any fruit juice into a popsicle, the recipes on the following pages take superfood alchemy one step further, incorporating celebrated anti-aging foods like cacao and maqui berry, and masterfully masking more "difficult" superfood ingredients like noni and spirulina.

 = FEATURED SUPERFOOD INGREDIENT

 QUICK REBOOT   DETOX & FLUSH    SLIM & TONE

 STRENGTH & STAMINA    BEAUTY & ANTI-AGING

CHOCOLATE-MINT NONI SOFT SERVE

Noni is not a polite flavor. If used carelessly, it barges in and takes over everything in its path with its potent "noni-ness," which tastes like a pungent overripe fruit. The key word to keep in mind when you are working with it in recipes is hide, hide, hide. This recipe blends delectable (but strong!) flavors to make a beautiful soft serve that, incredibly, manages to balance out noni's intensity quite successfully. This is a recipe where you will definitely not want to skip the agave, which helps keep noni's flavor in the background.

MAKES APPROXIMATELY 1 PINT

½ large avocado, pit and peel removed

⅓ cup agave nectar

½ cup cacao powder

1 cup coconut water

2 tablespoons noni juice

1 tablespoon vanilla extract

¼ teaspoon peppermint extract

¼ teaspoon guar gum (optional)

FEEL-GOOD FACT
Noni is loaded with antioxidants, and it boasts immune-boosting and tumor-fighting properties.

Blend all the ingredients together until very smooth. Transfer the mixture to a sealable shallow container, and place in the freezer until it is completely frozen—4–5 hours. (Alternatively, use an ice cream maker according to the manufacturer's directions for a fluffier frozen result.) Let soften for several minutes at room temperature before serving.

WHAT'S GUAR GUM?

Manufactured from an Indian bean known as the guar bean, or cluster bean, guar gum is generally sold as a white powder, and it is known to enhance the viscosity of recipes. It is a common natural ingredient in ice creams and frozen desserts because it lessens ice crystal formation, and ultimately produces smoother, creamier desserts. In small quantities guar gum does not affect flavor, but it can greatly enhance texture, so using it is an easy and natural way to practice a little molecular gastronomy. You can find guar gum in natural food stores, usually in the spice section or where gluten-free baking ingredients are stocked.

CARROT GINGER ICE CREAM

Before you judge this seemingly improbable combination, just try it. Once you do, I promise to share in your enthusiasm for Carrot Ginger Ice Cream and pretend you never raised an eyebrow.

MAKES APPROXIMATELY ONE PINT

10 carrots

1 inch fresh ginger root

½ cup raw cashews

¼ cup hemp seeds

¼ cup maple syrup

1 teaspoon vanilla extract

¼ teaspoon guar gum (optional)

⅓ cup crystallized ginger, chopped fine (optional)

Juice the carrots and fresh ginger. Pour the fresh-pressed juice into a blender and add the cashews, hemp seeds, maple syrup, vanilla, and guar gum. Blend well until smooth and creamy. Transfer the liquid into a sealable shallow container, and freeze for 1–2 hours. Mix the ice cream into a slushie, and fold in the crystallized ginger pieces. Return to the freezer for another 3–4 hours, or until frozen through. (Alternatively, use an ice cream maker according to the manufacturer's directions for a fluffier frozen result.) Let the ice cream defrost for a couple minutes to soften slightly at room temperature before serving.

JUICE BOOST
Add 1 teaspoon wheatgrass powder to the ice cream mix before freezing.

MASTER CLEANSE GRANITA

The "Master Cleanse" is a rather famous detox diet that is composed of drinking a concoction of water, lemon juice, grade B maple syrup, and cayenne pepper—and not much else— for several days at a time. Surprisingly, the flavor combination of the drink itself is quite satisfying. While I can't give this granita recipe the same sweeping health claims that the Master Cleanse broadcasts, I can say that it offers a mega-dose of vitamin C, is full of anti-inflammatory nutrients, and is uniquely delicious: cooling and spicy, sweet and tart.

MAKES APPROXIMATELY 1 QUART

4 apples, cored

½ inch fresh ginger root

2 lemons, juiced

⅓ cup grade B maple syrup

1 teaspoon camu berry powder

⅛ teaspoon cayenne powder

1 cup unflavored kombucha

¼ teaspoon guar gum (optional)

Juice the apples and the ginger root. Transfer the juice to a blender, and add the remaining ingredients. Blend just enough to fully incorporate the powders. Pour the mixture into a sealable shallow container, and freeze 4–6 hours longer, or until fully frozen. To serve, scrape the surface with the prongs of a fork to make "snow," and transfer to serving cups or glasses.

FEEL-GOOD FACT

Lemons are often used in liver and colon cleanses,
as they enhance both digestion and elimination.

CHERRY MERLOT GRANITA

"Leave no wine behind" is an underlying rule in my household, not that it needs much enforcement. Nevertheless, on the rare occasion when there is wine to spare, making this granita is a wonderful way to polish it off. Its dramatic, dark purple hue is a bold indicator of the potent anti-aging antioxidants in the cherries and aronia berries, and yes, even in the wine.

MAKES APPROXIMATELY 1 QUART

2 cups frozen pitted cherries

2 tablespoons aronia berry juice

1½ cups merlot, or other red wine

1 cup unflavored kombucha

½ teaspoon vanilla extract

sweetener, to taste

Add the cherries, aronia juice, merlot, kombucha, and vanilla extract to a blender, and blend for a quick moment just to mix. Add sweetener (such as stevia extract or agave nectar) to taste, and quickly blend once more—the mixture should be mostly blended, but with a few fruit chunks remaining. Pour the mixture into a sealable shallow container and freeze until solid (about 4–6 hours). To serve, scrape the surface with the prongs of a fork to make a deep purple "snow," and transfer to serving bowls.

VARIATION
Use a tablespoon of acai berry powder or a teaspoon of maqui berry powder in place of the aronia berry juice.

CANTALOUPE SEA BUCKTHORN GRANITA

A little bit of agave helps to give the cantaloupe and citrus flavors the brightness they deserve in this granita, but stevia can help finish the job, while keeping the overall sugar content low. The vibrant flavors of the ice combined with its simplicity are the essence of faux-fancy.

MAKES APPROXIMATELY 3 CUPS

½ cantaloupe, seeds and peel discarded

2 limes, juiced

1 Meyer lemon, juiced

3 tablespoons sea buckthorn berry juice

2 tablespoons agave nectar

½ teaspoon ground white or black pepper

¼ teaspoon guar gum (optional)

sweetener, to taste

Combine the cantaloupe flesh and juice with the lime juice, lemon juice, sea buckthorn berry juice, agave nectar, and white or black pepper. Blend until smooth. Taste, and add additional sweetener (stevia, or the sweetener of your choice) until slightly oversweet (it will balance out when it's frozen). Transfer the mixture to a sealable shallow container. Freeze for 1–2 hours, then remove from the freezer and stir with a fork to break the ice crystals apart and make a slush. Freeze for 2–3 hours longer, or until frozen through. To serve, scrape the surface with the prongs of a fork to make snow, and transfer to serving cups or glasses.

FEEL-GOOD FACT

Sea Buckthorn is often thought of as a beauty superfood. Its abundance of carotenoid antioxidants, vitamin E, vitamin C, and omega fatty acids are a dream team of potent nutrition to support healthy skin and hair.

RASPBERRY GRANITA

Raspberries help bring out the subtle flavor of the maqui in this light and beautiful granita, which could make a unique breakfast on a hot day just as easily as a special dessert.

MAKES APPROXIMATELY 1 QUART

- 1½ cups raspberries
- 3 cups red seedless grapes
- 2 Meyer lemons, juiced
- 2 teaspoons maqui berry powder
- 2 tablespoons liquid sweetener, like agave
- ¼ teaspoon guar gum (optional)

Juice the raspberries and grapes. Pour the juice into a blender, and add the Meyer lemon juice, maqui powder, and liquid sweetener of your choice. Blend well, then pour the contents into a sealable shallow container. Freeze until solid (about 4–6 hours). To serve, scrape the surface with the prongs of a fork to form a red "snow," and transfer to serving bowls.

....

FEEL-GOOD FACT
Whenever possible, use red grapes instead of green or white grapes; you'll consume around 12% more antioxidants just by enjoying the darker varieties.

....

MAQUI PEAR KOMBUCHA SORBET

Delicate and light, this tranquil sorbet offers a refreshing sweetness without being overwhelming. Stevia may be used in place of agave nectar for an even lower calorie treat; you'll want to sweeten to a level that is slightly "oversweet," which will balance out once the ingredients are frozen.

MAKES APPROXIMATELY 1 QUART

4 very ripe pears, cored

1 lemon, juiced

1½ cups unflavored kombucha

3 tablespoons agave nectar

2 tablespoons maqui berry powder

¼ teaspoon guar gum (optional)

First, juice the pears. In a pitcher, combine the fresh pear juice with the lemon juice, kombucha, agave, and maqui, and stir well. Transfer the mixture to a sealable shallow container, cover tightly, and freeze for 1 hour. Remove from the freezer, and use a fork to scrape and "fluff" up the ice crystals, mixing them into a slush. Freeze for 3–4 hours longer, or until sorbet is frozen through and firm. An ice cream maker can also be used to produce a fluffier result.

> ### JUICE BOOST
> Add 2 tablespoons mangosteen juice for
> a wider variety of antioxidants.

POMEGRANATE-ACAI GRANITA

No need to break out the juicer: You're off the hook here on this extra-simple recipe. Fresh pomegranate seeds add a welcome texture to this delicate, gorgeous Italian ice.

MAKES APPROXIMATELY 3 CUPS

2 cups pomegranate juice

3 tablespoons acai powder

2 tablespoons maple syrup

¼ teaspoon cinnamon powder

pinch cayenne powder

¼ teaspoon guar gum (optional)

1 cup pomegranate seeds

Blend together the pomegranate juice, acai, maple syrup, cinnamon, cayenne, and guar gum. Pour the mixture into a sealable shallow container. Freeze for 1–2 hours, then remove from the freezer and stir with a fork to break the ice crystals apart and make a slush. Freeze for 2–3 hours longer, or until frozen through. To serve, scrape the surface with the prongs of a fork to form a ruby-red snow, gently toss with fresh pomegranate seeds, and transfer to serving cups or glasses.

JUICE BOOST
Blend in 1 cup fresh or frozen blueberries before freezing.

GREEN FRUIT POPS

Fun for kids (and adults!), these green pops are a great way to incorporate the power of green superfoods in a treat-like manner.

MAKES APPROXIMATELY 1 QUART (ABOUT 10 3-OUNCE POPSICLES)

2 apples, cored

6 large kale leaves

1 teaspoon spirulina powder

2 very ripe bananas

sweetener, to taste

Juice the apples and the kale. Transfer the juice to a blender, add the spirulina and bananas, then blend until smooth. Adjust the sweetness (using stevia extract or other desired sweetener) until just slightly "too sweet," as the sweetness will diminish a bit when frozen. Pour the mixture into popsicle molds, and freeze until solid (about 4–6 hours).

FEEL-GOOD FACT

Just 1 tablespoon of spirulina powder has 15 milligrams of iron—500% more than a 3-ounce serving of beef.

CHIA FRESCAS

In about 20 minutes, chia seeds transform from small crunchy seeds to slippery textural treats when combined with juice . . . creating a "chia fresca." A classic drink hailing from Mexico, chia frescas are traditionally served with a citrus juice and sweetener. Here, chia's special quality plays an exciting role with various superfood juices that offer a wide range of flavor and nutrition. Although you can add chia seeds to make a quasi-fresca out of virtually any juice, the recipes that follow (which put everything from superberries to healthy greens to use) create particularly delectable results.

 = FEATURED SUPERFOOD INGREDIENT

QUICK REBOOT   DETOX & FLUSH   SLIM & TONE

  STRENGTH & STAMINA   BEAUTY & ANTI-AGING

CRANBERRY-ORANGE CHIA FRESCA

Between the high levels of anti-aging vitamin C and rejuvenating omega fats, this punch-like fresca is a dream for promoting beautiful skin. Using a no-sugar sweetener like stevia to balance the tartness of the cranberry juice is a smart way to keep the nutrient density high and the calories (and sugar) down.

MAKES APPROXIMATELY 1 QUART

4 large Navel oranges

½-inch fresh ginger (optional)

1 cup unsweetened pure cranberry juice

1 tablespoon sea buckthorn berry juice

¼ cup chia seeds

1–2 cups unflavored kombucha

sweetener, to taste

Juice the oranges and ginger. In a quart-sized mason jar or other large container with a lid, combine the fresh juice with the cranberry juice, sea buckthorn berry juice, and chia seeds. Fill the remainder of the container with kombucha, seal, and shake well. Taste, and mix in a little stevia (or other sweetener) as desired. Let sit for 10 minutes to allow the chia seeds to swell. Shake vigorously to separate any seed clumps, then let sit for 10 minutes longer. The mixture will keep for several days, refrigerated.

FEEL-GOOD FACT
Chia seeds contain 8 times more omega-3 fatty acids than salmon.

ELECTROLYTE CHIA LEMONADE

This "lemonade" is a staple that I make in bulk and keep in the fridge, so it's ready whenever thirst strikes; plus the electrolytes and anti-inflammatory nutrients (omega-3s and vitamin C) make it absolutely perfect, pre- and post-exercise.

MAKES 16 OUNCES

1 cup coconut water

1 cup filtered water

2 tablespoons chia seeds

1 tablespoon fresh lemon juice

½ lemon, sliced into thin rounds

sweetener, to taste

In a shaker cup or sealable jar, combine the coconut water, filtered water, chia seeds, and lemon juice, then stir or shake very well to keep mixture from clumping. Add the lemon slices and shake once more. Let the mixture rest for 15–20 minutes until chia seeds are saturated. Shake the beverage once more, and sweeten to taste using stevia or desired sweetener. Best served cold, over ice.

JUICE BOOST
Add a spoonful of acai powder.

POMEGRANATE CHIA FRESCA

Although superfood juices don't get much easier, this is, in fact, an incredibly symbiotic recipe: The high vitamin C content of the pomegranate juice helps make the impressive iron content of the chia seeds more bioavailable to the body, and the fiber and omega fats in the chia seeds help slow down the release of the juice's natural sugars into the bloodstream to promote more sustainable energy. What a beautiful pairing!

MAKES APPROXIMATELY 16 OUNCES

- 1¾ cups pomegranate juice
- ¼ cup chia seeds

In a shaker cup or sealable jar, combine the pomegranate juice and chia seeds, then stir or shake the mixture very well in order to break apart the seeds and avoid clumping. Let the beverage rest for 15–20 minutes, then shake it once more and serve cold, over ice.

VARIATION
Other vitamin C rich juices, such as cranberry, orange, or grapefruit may easily be substituted for the pomegranate juice.

GREEN APPLE KALE CHIA FRESCA

My friend couldn't help but pull a sassy challenge of "oh no you didn't" on me when I shared my excitement over this green recipe with her, as we both vehemently believe kale and chia are two of the best things ever. I encourage you to try this empowering drink when you want a delicious dose of "oh yes I did." This drink is best served lightly sweetened and over ice.

MAKES APPROXIMATELY 1 QUART

2 cups filtered water

3 tablespoons chia seeds

2 large green apples, cored

½ inch fresh ginger root

4 kale leaves

1 lemon, juiced

sweetener, to taste

In a shaker cup, combine the water and chia seeds, and shake well. Refrigerate the mixture for 10 minutes to allow the chia seeds to swell. Shake vigorously to separate any seed clumps, then continue to refrigerate for a minimum of 10 minutes longer to form a gel. Juice the apples, ginger, and kale leaves; then mix in the lemon juice. Shake the gelled chia once more, then mix in the fresh juice. Taste, add a little stevia (or other sweetener) as desired, and shake one last time to fully incorporate the juice with the plumped chia seeds. Serve over ice; it will keep for several days, refrigerated.

FEEL-GOOD FACT
Kale is a particularly good source of vitamin K, which is important for bone health, cancer protection, and many other bodily functions.

ACAI BERRY CHIA FRESCA

This is a filling acai and chia drink that is an unbelievable source of sustainable energy. Due to its naturally sweet nature, this is a great drink for kids, who often enjoy the unique texture of soaked chia seeds just as much as adults!

MAKES APPROXIMATELY 1 QUART

3 cups strawberries

4 cups red seedless grapes

1 Meyer lemon, juiced

1½ tablespoons acai powder

3 tablespoons chia seeds

Juice the strawberries and grapes. Pour the juice into a quart-sized mason jar or other large container with a lid, and add the Meyer lemon juice, acai powder, and chia seeds. Seal the jar and shake very well. Let sit for 10 minutes to allow the chia seeds to swell, shake vigorously to separate any seed clumps, then let sit for 10 minutes longer. Will keep for several days, refrigerated

JUICE BOOST
Juice a handful of spinach while juicing the fresh fruit.

HONEYDEW MINT CHIA FRESCA

I am always immediately drawn to fresh melon drinks—to me, their cooling flavor is unsurpassed in the refreshing department, which means they're an ideal base for chia frescas.

MAKES APPROXIMATELY 1 QUART

1 honeydew melon, seeds and rind removed

2 cucumbers

2 handfuls fresh mint

½ teaspoon wheatgrass powder

2 tablespoons chia seeds

sweetener, to taste

Juice the melon, cucumbers, and mint. Transfer the juice to a quart-sized mason jar or other large container with a lid, add the wheatgrass powder and chia seeds, and shake very well. Taste, and mix in a little stevia (or other sweetener) as desired. Let sit for 10 minutes to allow the chia seeds to swell, shake vigorously to separate any seed clumps, then let sit for 10 minutes longer. The mixture will keep for several days, refrigerated.

JUICE BOOST

In addition to giving chia frescas like this one a beautiful emerald color, liquid chlorophyll is highly alkaline and has the power to help rebuild and replenish red blood cells. If you can find mint chlorophyll drops (where the concentrate is partially derived from fresh mint), they'd make a great addition to this juice.

SPRITZERS & INFUSIONS

The beauty of spritzers and infusions is that they act as low-calorie, low-sugar beverages (compared to pure juice). Superfood spritzers are made by combining kombucha with fresh juice (kombucha can also be substituted with mineral water or another effervescent beverage), while infusions are created by steeping whole food ingredients to extract flavor (just as you would with tea). No matter which method you choose, exciting new flavors and aromas can be achieved, and virtually anything from kale to goji berries can be used. Use the recipes in this section as a springboard to customize your own spritzer and infusion creations.

= FEATURED SUPERFOOD INGREDIENT

QUICK REBOOT   DETOX & FLUSH   SLIM & TONE

STRENGTH & STAMINA   BEAUTY & ANTI-AGING

MANDARIN GINGER KOMBUCHA SPRITZER

As if an ordinary orange isn't enough of a fruity gem, mandarin oranges take the idea of sweet citrus to candy-like heights. Juicing these small beauties produces an irresistible nectar, enriched here with extra vitamin C from camu and warming ginger.

MAKES APPROXIMATELY 1 QUART

2 large sweet apples, cored

10 mandarin oranges, peeled

1 inch fresh ginger root

1 teaspoon camu berry powder

2 cups unflavored or ginger kombucha

JUICE BOOST
Blend 2 tablespoons dried goji berries into the juice.

Juice the apples, mandarin oranges, and ginger root. Transfer the juice to a shaker cup or blender, add the camu berry powder, and blend well to combine. Fill serving glasses halfway with juice, and top with kombucha.

THE NEW POP CULTURE: KOMBUCHA

Sure, kombucha's a little strange looking, but that hasn't stopped this fizzy elixir from becoming one of the leading beverages in the health field. Don't let its soda pop-like effervescence fool you: kombucha is a very special type of fermented tea that offers a refreshing taste, an energizing boost, and detoxifying benefits. Full of live enzymes and vitamins, kombucha is one the healthiest ways to enjoy a bubbly beverage—making it a refreshing companion for fresh superfood juices. You can find kombucha at health food stores all across North America in the refrigerated beverage section, and it can even be made at home for just a few pennies and a little patience.

MAQUI-GRAPEFRUIT KOMBUCHA SPRITZER

A purple-powered, mimosa-esque delight with just a little kick, this is next-level kombucha, for sure.

MAKES APPROXIMATELY 18 OUNCES

1 large grapefruit, peeled

1 inch fresh ginger root

1 teaspoon maqui berry powder

1 cup unflavored kombucha

Juice the grapefruit and ginger. Mix in the maqui powder until well combined, then add the kombucha.

FEEL-GOOD FACT

Maqui contains more anthocyanin antioxidants, famous for their anti-aging benefits, than any fruit discovered.

PINEAPPLE CILANTRO KOMBUCHA SPRITZER

Pineapple-based juices have a friendly tartness, which makes cilantro's clean flavor seem extra fresh-tasting. This spritzer is rather light on kombucha (the "spritz"); additional kombucha can be added to elevate the effervescence.

MAKES APPROXIMATELY 1 QUART

1 pineapple, top and peel removed

1 cucumber

1 green apple, cored

1 large handful spinach

1 small handful cilantro

8 ounces unflavored or ginger kombucha, or more to taste

½ lime, juiced

sweetener, to taste

Juice all the produce. Pour the juice into a pitcher and stir in the kombucha and lime juice. Taste, and sweeten with stevia (or desired sweetener) to maximize flavor. Add additional kombucha if needed.

JUICE BOOST
Add 2 tablespoons mangosteen juice to the fresh juice mixture.

GREEN TEA GOJI INFUSION

Okay, you caught me. I totally included a recipe with the same flavor combination in one of my other books, Superfood Smoothies, *but this version pays homage to traditional Chinese methods of steeping goji berries in tea. Adding a little bit of (non-traditional) cucumber juice to the mix enhances the cleansing properties of this special drink. Bonus: The plumped goji berries are a delicious treat at the bottom of the glass.*

MAKES APPROXIMATELY 1 QUART

2 cups brewed green tea

⅓ cup goji berries

2 cucumbers

1 inch fresh ginger root

sweetener, to taste (optional)

mint leaves, for garnish

In a pitcher, combine the green tea and goji berries. Let stand for 20–30 minutes, or until goji berries have hydrated and become plump. Juice the cucumbers and ginger root; then stir the fresh juice into the goji berry infusion. Sweeten with stevia (or other desired sweetener) if needed. Add a handful of fresh mint leaves and serve chilled.

FEEL-GOOD FACT
Because it increases thermogenesis (an important part of metabolism), green tea is an excellent tool for weight loss: It promotes fat burning, regulates blood sugar levels, and increases energy.

BLUEBERRY PEACH AGUA FRESCA

The dynamic duo of blueberries and peaches is usually reserved for summer months, but you can enjoy these fruits year-round in an agua fresca, like this one, if you use frozen fruit.

MAKES APPROXIMATELY ½ GALLON

1 cup frozen blueberries

2 cups frozen sliced peaches

1 cinnamon stick

½ gallon filtered water

sweetener, to taste (optional)

Place the fruit and cinnamon in a large pitcher, pour the water on top, and refrigerate for a minimum of 2 hours. Sweeten to taste using stevia (or other sweetener), if desired. Best served strained and over ice. This fresca will keep for several days, refrigerated.

VARIATION
Add a couple jasmine tea bags instead of cinnamon to the water and let slowly steep for several hours.

STRAWBERRY LIME AGUA FRESCA

Agua fresca is translated as "fresh water." It is very light in taste and made from filtered water that has been flavorfully infused with slices of fruit, herbs, and even flowers. You won't need a juicer for this type of recipe, since the action of osmosis releases the juice from the produce organically. I like to incorporate frozen fruit in agua frescas to intensify flavors even more.

MAKES APPROXIMATELY ½ GALLON

2 cups frozen strawberries

2 limes, sliced thin

½ gallon filtered water

sweetener, to taste (optional)

Place the fruit in a large pitcher, pour the water on top, and refrigerate for a minimum of 2 hours. Sweeten to taste using stevia (or other sweetener), if desired. Best served strained and over ice. This fresca will keep for several days, refrigerated.

VARIATION
Replace up to ⅓ of the water with fresh cucumber juice.

SUPERFOOD COCKTAILS

Many of the superfood juice recipes in this book can easily be used to make incredible cocktails, with the simple addition of wine, beer, or spirits. If alcohol is something you enjoy, why not make the most out of your drink and get in a few nutrients at the same time? Almost any cocktail is a superfood opportunity, as you'll see in these delicious, clean cocktail recipes that celebrate superfoods such as mangosteen, strawberries, and even detoxifying wheatgrass. Of course, cocktails can easily be made into mocktails—just use unflavored kombucha instead of the alcohol.

 = FEATURED SUPERFOOD INGREDIENT

 QUICK REBOOT   DETOX & FLUSH   SLIM & TONE

 STRENGTH & STAMINA    BEAUTY & ANTI-AGING

STRAWBERRY WINE SPRITZER

Oh, do I love a good glass of wine, which I believe should be smiled upon and savored, completely unadulterated. But when it's just a bottom-shelf-wine-Wednesday, my preferred way of imbibing is to mix wine with kombucha. Because of its effervescence, kombucha creates a spritzer-like effect, and since kombucha helps detoxify the liver (one of its many benefits), it actually helps counterbalance a bit of the less-than-ideal effects wine has on the body. A small addition of potent superfood juice turns the mixture into a completely celebratory cocktail ... whether it's a discount-wine-Wednesday or even a fully fancy-wine-Friday.

MAKES APPROXIMATELY 1 QUART

4 cups strawberries

1½ cups light white wine (such as pinot grigio, sauvignon blanc, or other dry whites)

1½ cups unflavored or ginger kombucha

sweetener, to taste

Juice the strawberries. In a pitcher, combine the juice, white wine, and kombucha together and stir. Sweeten with stevia (or other desired sweetener) if needed. Serve chilled, over ice.

JUICE BOOST
Mix in 1 tablespoon aronia berry juice to raise the antioxidant content.

BLOOD ORANGE
& SEA BUCKTHORN MIMOSA

Blood oranges, with their appealing ruby-colored hue, make mimosas appear extra special, and sea buckthorn berry juice gives the mix a subtle honey flavor. An added bonus from sea buckthorn: skin-rejuvenating nutrients. If blood oranges aren't in season, use another orange variety like Valencia (substituting will not affect the flavor).

MAKES APPROXIMATELY 1 QUART

6 medium blood oranges, peeled

2 tablespoons sea buckthorn berry juice

2 cups champagne, chilled

Juice the blood oranges and mix with sea buckthorn berry juice. Fill champagne glasses halfway with juice, then top with champagne.

JUICE BOOST
Add 1 teaspoon maqui berry powder to the mixture.

MANGOSTEEN PEACH SAKE SANGRIA

Sake takes on flavors remarkably well, which makes it an ideal base for the lightly sweet and floral qualities of mangosteen and peaches. Using frozen instead of fresh peaches infuses this cocktail with extra-fruity flavor.

MAKES APPROXIMATELY 2 QUARTS

2 cups frozen peaches

1 24-ounce bottle cold sake (rice wine)

1 16-ounce bottle ginger kombucha

⅓ cup mangosteen juice

sweetener, to taste (optional)

In a pitcher, mix together the frozen peaches, sake, kombucha, and mangosteen juice. Refrigerate for 1–2 hours, or until the peaches have fully defrosted and are soft. Sweeten with stevia (or other desired sweetener) if needed. Serve chilled, over ice.

JUICE BOOST

Add ¼ cup dried goji berries along with the frozen fruit, which will plump up nicely after being soaked for an hour in the sangria.

HONEYDEW WHEATGRASS MARGARITA

This margarita is almost a little "too good," if you get my drift. It's hydrating, cooling, naturally sweet, and secretly packed with detoxifying wheatgrass powder (though you'd never know it). If you'd prefer a blended drink (versus serving it on the rocks), try freezing coconut water in an ice cube tray ahead of time to make "coconut ice." This way, as your drink melts, the flavor will not be watered down.

MAKES APPROXIMATELY 1 QUART

½ honeydew melon, seeds and rind removed

1 teaspoons fresh lime zest

1 lime, juiced

1 cup coconut water

1 teaspoon wheatgrass powder

4 ounces white tequila

ice

Juice the melon. Pour the fresh juice into a blender, and add the lime zest, lime juice, coconut water, wheatgrass powder, and tequila; blend to combine. Serve on the rocks or blend with ice. Garnish with a lime wedge and a sprinkle of additional lime zest.

FEEL-GOOD FACT
As a premium supplier of chlorophyll, wheatgrass neutralizes toxins in the body, and helps purify the liver.

KALE MARTINI

This chic little green number isn't just for health nuts; it can easily stand its ground with the most sophisticated drinks. Agave nectar offers a more balanced drink, but if you are looking to cut sugar and calories even further, stevia extract is a good substitute for some (or all) of the syrup.

MAKES APPROXIMATELY 1½ CUPS (4 MARTINIS)

6 kale leaves

2 cucumbers

ice

2 limes, juiced

¼ cup agave nectar

4 ounces vodka

cucumber slices or baby kale leaves, for garnish

Juice the kale and the cucumbers. Pour into a mixing glass filled with ice. Add the lime juice, agave, and vodka. Stir for 30 seconds, then strain into martini glasses. Garnish with a cucumber slice or baby kale leaf.

JUICE BOOST
Add a few drops of chlorella extract to boost the chlorophyll content of the juice and enhance its green hue.

PART THREE

EXTRAS

SUPERFOOD SUBSTITUTION CHEAT SHEET

While every superfood ingredient has its own alchemy of nutrition to offer,
juice recipes are exceptionally forgiving when it comes to substitutions.
Results may vary per recipe – adjust the quantity and flavor to taste.
Note that some substitutions are non-superfood ingredients.

SUPERFOOD		SUBSTITUTION
Acai Berry Powder	=	Maqui Berry Powder (use half as much)
Aronia Berry Juice	=	Unsweetened Pure Cranberry Juice
Burdock Root	=	Omit from recipe
Cacao Powder	=	Cocoa Powder
Camu Berry Powder	=	Omit from recipe
Fresh Greens	=	Multi-greens Powder (use to taste)
Hemp Seeds	=	Raw Sunflower Seeds
Lucuma Powder	=	Oat Flour, or omit from recipe
Mangosteen Juice	=	Peach Juice
Noni Juice	=	Omit from recipe
Pomegranate Juice	=	Cranberry Juice
Sea Buckthorn Berry Juice	=	Orange Juice (Use at least double the amount)
Spirulina Powder	=	Chlorella Powder (use half as much), or omit from recipe
Strawberries	=	Raspberries
Wheatgrass	=	Fresh parsley (small handful)

CONVERSION CHART

NON-LIQUID INGREDIENTS (Weights of common ingredients in grams)

INGREDIENT	1 CUP	¾ CUP	⅔ CUP	½ CUP	⅓ CUP	¼ CUP	2 TBSP
Chia Seeds	163 g	122 g	108 g	81 g	54 g	41 g	20 g
Chopped fruits and vegetables	150 g	110 g	100 g	75 g	50 g	40 g	20 g
Goji berries	111 g	83 g	74 g	55 g	37 g	28 g	14 g
Nuts, chopped	150 g	110 g	100 g	75 g	50 g	40 g	20 g

Note: Non-liquid ingredients specified in American recipes by volume (if more than about 2 tablespoons or 1 fluid ounce) can be converted to weight with the table above. If you need to convert an ingredient that isn't in this table, the safest thing to do is to measure it with a traditional measuring cup and then weigh the results with a metric scale. In a pinch, you can use the volume conversion table below.

VOLUME CONVERSIONS
(USED FOR LIQUIDS)

CUSTOMARY QUANTITY	METRIC EQUIVALENT
1 teaspoon	5 mL
1 tablespoon or ½ fluid ounce	15 mL
¼ cup or 2 fluid ounces	60 mL
⅓ cup	80 mL
½ cup or 4 fluid ounces	120 mL
⅔ cup	160 mL
1 cup or 8 fluid ounces or ½ pint	250 mL
1½ cups or 12 fluid ounces	350 mL
2 cups or 1 pint or 16 fluid ounces	475 mL
3 cups or 1½ pints	700 mL

FREQUENTLY ASKED QUESTIONS

What's the difference between a smoothie and a juice?

Smoothies are blended beverages made from (mostly) whole foods. A juice is like a smoothie except has had its fibrous mass removed. Each has its benefits: smoothies are often more satiating, and a little faster to prepare, while juices are more concentrated in micronutrients and more detoxifying.

How much juice should I drink (what is considered "a serving")?

Most people find that 12–16 ounces of juice is a satiating amount of juice. This quantity is flexible based upon your size, metabolism, activity level, current health status, as well as the variety of juice (such as a fruit-based chia fresca versus an all-vegetable green drink). Pay attention to your individual needs, and listen to the way your body responds. What "works" for one person may be different than what works for you . . . and that's more than okay.

I have never heard of (or seen) some of these superfood ingredients before. Where do I find them?

Most health food stores (and even a few conventional grocery stores) sell all of the superfood ingredients listed in this book—yes, even sea buckthorn berry juice and spirulina powder! If you don't live near a store that carries these products, ordering them online is an extremely easy, no-hassle route. See page 203 for a directory of my personal favorite, most trusted companies, or do a quick search online to scout the most current deals on these products.

Do I have to buy all of the products you list in the book?

Absolutely not. I include a carefully selected range of incredible superfoods to choose from as a way to inspire new culinary adventures and promote increased health and wellness gains. However, keep in mind these are functional ingredients, and there is no need to incorporate all of these superfoods all of the time. Instead, select the superfoods that offer the benefits you are most looking to acquire, and start there with the juices that incorporate them. Try adding one or two new ingredients each month—rotating ingredients is not only acceptable, it's encouraged. You can also refer to the substitution chart on page 199 if you don't have a superfood ingredient required for a recipe.

What's the best superfood to start with for "boosting" fresh juices?

I always recommend fresh leafy greens—from kale to parsley—as the first class of superfoods we should all look to consume more of (in any form but especially in juices). Beyond these, an ideal "starter" superfood juice ingredient is wheatgrass powder—its mild flavor makes it wildly adaptable, and it instantly catapults the nourishment as well as the detoxifying potential of any kind of juice.

Are there any ways to cut down the cost of juicing?

Juicing is admittedly not the most inexpensive habit, yet keep in mind a homemade juice—even with all its superfood additions—is usually half or even a third of the price of a fresh-pressed one purchased at a juice bar or restaurant (which usually range from $6–$12).To cut costs, make juices with seasonal produce, shop at farmer's markets, and look for discounts on pantry superfood items online. Though the initial purchase may seem steep, specialty superfood powders and juice concentrates last a very long time (aka for many, many juices!) thanks to their condensed nutrition and small serving size.

When we look to purchase nutrients, not calories, when food shopping, superfoods are not as expensive as they seem. For example, you'd have to buy over 8 oranges (approximately $5.00) to get the vitamin C content of 1 teaspoon of camu berry powder (approximately $0.54).

What's the best way to store superfood ingredients?

Fresh superfood ingredients like green kale should be stored in the crisper drawer of the refrigerator. Superfood seeds like chia and hemp will last longer when refrigerated. Powdered and dried superfood ingredients can remain in a cool, dry place in the kitchen away from direct sunlight, but will last longer if kept in the refrigerator (in particular, acai powder). Refer to the product packaging for expiration dates.

What kind of juicer do you use?

I have a Breville Juice Fountain Duo, which was used for all the recipe development for this book, and is my personal home juicer of choice. See pages 30–31 for more information on juicers.

Is there anything I can do with all this juice pulp?

Anyone who juices regularly knows there's a lot of "pulp," or fibrous produce mass, that's left over from the process of juicing. You certainly can use this in recipes, and it usually lasts a couple days refrigerated. Add a little to smoothies or soups for extra fiber, mix a couple spoonfuls into baked treats to add moisture, or even blend with nuts and seeds and bake at a low temperature into "crackers." My favorite use of pulp? Compost. Juice pulp makes incredible compost because it's already partially broken down plant-matter, and I love that it eventually becomes part of my home vegetable garden again. Also, I personally feel that eating the pulp defeats the point of juicing a little from a nutrition standpoint—if a person goes to the trouble of juicing a carrot, then baking its pulp into crackers and eating those too... why not just eat the whole carrot in the first place and save yourself the trouble? (Aside from a fun culinary experience, of course.) Regardless, whether you incorporate the pulp into recipes or into the soil, it's all a good thing.

Ingredients

NAVITAS NATURALS
Specializes in organic superfoods and more
Find here: Acai powder, Cacao powder, Camu berry powder, Chia seeds, Dried goji berries, Goji berry powder, Goldenberry Powder, Hemp seeds, Lucuma powder, Maca powder, Maqui powder, Raw cashews, Wheatgrass powder
Visit: Navitasnaturals.com

GENESIS TODAY
Offers superfood juices, greens powder, and other superfood products
Find here: Mangosteen juice, Noni juice, Sea buckthorn berry juice, GenEssentials Greens* (a greens powder blend)
Visit: Genesistoday.com

SUPERBERRIES
Specializes in aronia berry products
Find here: Aronia berry juice
Visit: Superberries.com

NUTREX-HAWAII
Specializes in Spirulina
Find here: Spirulina Powder
Visit: Nutrex-hawaii.com

VEGA
Offers recommended flavored protein powder (top-quality ingredients, assimilates very easily into juices, and tastes good) and source for chlorella powder
Find here: Chlorella powder, Performance Protein Powder* (Vanilla recommended)
Visit: Myvega.com

MANITOBA HARVEST
Specializes in hemp foods and oils, including hemp protein powder
Find here: Hemp Pro 70* (a high-protein, water-soluble hemp protein powder that works incredibly well in juices as an unflavored, unsweetened protein)
Visit: Manitobaharvest.com

HERBS, ETC.
Offers a large variety of herbal products
Find here: ChlorOxygen chlorophyll drops*
Visit: Herbsetc.com

NUNATURALS
Carries stevia products
Find here: Liquid, powdered, and even flavored stevia
Visit: Nunaturals.com

MOUNTAIN ROSE HERBS
A source for buying bulk organic herbs and spices
Find here: A variety of culinary and medicinal herbs and spices, such as cinnamon and rose
Visit: Mountainroseherbs.com

Kitchen Tools

BREVILLE
High quality kitchen equipment, including Superfood Juices recommended juicer
Find here: Juice Fountain* juicers (The recipes in this book were all created and tested in a Juice Fountain Duo machine), and wheatgrass juicer (Juice Fountain Crush*)
Visit: Brevilleusa.com

OXO
Find here: Ice cube trays with lids, stainless steel mesh strainers, manual citrus squeezer
Visit: Oxo.com

TOVOLO
Find here: BPA-free, silicon ice cube trays
Visit: Tovolo.com

GLASS DHARMA
Find here: Reusable glass drinking straws
Visit: Glassdharma.com

AMAZON
Find here: Almost any tool or shelf-stable ingredient you can't find in a store or online, such as nut milk bags, cheesecloth, specialty powders, etc . . . often for a discounted price.
Visit: Amazon.com

*Indicates brand-name ingredient

REFERENCES

"A randomized, double-blind, placebo-controlled clinical study of the general effects of a standardized Lyciumbarbarium (Goji) juice, GoChi." *ncbi.hlm.nih.gov*. National Center for Biotechnology Information, May 2008.

Bittman, Mark. *Leafy Greens*. New York, NY: Macmillan, 1995.

Clum, Dr. Lauren, and Snyder, Dr. Mariza. *The Antioxidant Counter.* Berkley, CA: Ulysses Press, 2011.

Coates, Wayne, PhD. *Chia: The Complete Guide to the Ultimate Superfood.* New York, NY: Sterling, 2012.

Davis, Brenda, RD, and Vesanto Melina, MS, RD, and Rynn Berry. *Becoming Raw: The Essential Guide to Raw Vegan Diets.* Summertown, TN: Book Publishing Company, 2010.

Hardy, Connie. "Aronia Berries Profile." AGMRC.org. Agricultural Marketing Resource Center, June 2012.

Ley, Beth M., Ph.D. *Maca: Adaptogen and Hormonal Regulator.* Detroit Lakes, MN: BL Publications, 2003.

"Maca." *mskcc.org*. Memorial Sloan-Kettering Cancer Center, April 2013.

"Mangosteen." *mskcc.org*. Memorial Sloan-Kettering Cancer Center, May 2013.

"Noni: Science and Safety." *nccam.nih.gov*. National Center for Complementary and Alternative Medicine, Apr 2012.

"Omega 7: The new superstar fatty acid." *Timespub.com*. Times Publishing Newspapers, Feb 2013.

Page, Linda, Ph.D. *Linda page's 12th Edition Healthy Healing: A Guide to Self-Healing for Everyone.* Healthy Healing, Inc., 2004.

"Phytochemicals and Cardiovascular Disease." *heart.org*. American Heart Association, May 2013.

"Pomegranate Ellagitannin-Derived Compounds Exhibit Antiproliferative and Antiaromatase Activity in Breast Cancer Cells *In vitro.*" *cancerpreventionresearch.aacrjournals. org*. American Association for Cancer Prevention Research. July 2009.

"Prostate Cancer, Nutrition, and Dietary Supplements." *cancer.gov*. National Cancer Institute.

Raloff, Janet. "Chocolate as Sunscreen," *sciencenews.org*. Science News. June 2006.

Raloff, Janet. "Prescription Strength Chocolate, Revisited." *sciencenews.org*. Science News, Feb 2006.

"Strawberries, blueberries can boost a woman's heart health: study." *nydailynews.com*. New York Daily News, Jan 2013.

"Strawberries Can Help Protect Skin From UVA Rays." *medicalnewstoday.com*. Medical News Today, Aug 2012.

Tahseen, Ismat. "Eat purple cabbage for great skin." *Indiatimes.com*. The Times of India, Feb 2013.

"The Best Antioxidants and Superfoods." *oracvalues.com*. ORAC Values.

Vartan, Starre. "Discovered: Indian spice reduces Alzheimer's symptoms by 30%." *MNN.com*. Mother Nature Network, July 2010.

"Vitamin C and Skin Health." Linus Pauling Institute at Oregon State University. http://lpi.oregonstate.edu/infocenter/skin/vitaminC/index.html.

Vozzola, Lauren. "Purslane: A weed worth eating." *Chicagotribune.com*. The Chicago Tribune, 2013.

"Watercress: Anti-Cancer Superfood." *medicalnewstoday.com*. Medical News Today, Feb 2007.

Wolfe, David. *Superfoods: The Food and Medicine of the Future.* Berkley, CA: North Atalantic Books, 2009.

Zeb, Alam. "Chemical and Nutritional Constituents of Sea Buckthorn Juice," *pjbs.org*. Pakistan Journal of Nutrition, 2004.

Zelman, Kathleen M., MPH, RD, LD. "The Truth About Kale: Nutrition, Recipe Ideas, and More." *webMD.com*. WebMD, 2010.

ACKNOWLEDGMENTS

I feel incredibly fortunate to be surrounded by such a strong, fun, and talented team of friends, loved ones and collaborators who, together, helped make this book extremely special.

An enormous thank you to Oliver Barth for making these pages come alive with all of your jaw-dropping (and mouth-watering) photography. The love that was put in each of them shines through, and I cherish the time spent creating with you . . . with all my heart.

Thank you to my wonderful family, Mom, Dad and Nama for instilling a sense of value in creativity since day one. It's because of you that I'm able to use the word "work" and "dream" in the same sentence. Your support and love means so much to me.

Speaking of dreams, thank you to the definition of "dream team" at Sterling for publishing this project so beautifully. Thank you to Jennifer Williams for being such a wonderful caretaker of the words on these pages—I feel lucky to be able to call you my editor and adore you. Thank you to Christine Heun for the flawless design that graces this book. Thank you to Elizabeth Mihaltse for all your talents and care in creating such an alluring cover. And thank you Kim Marini for steering the ship and keeping everything on track!

Thank you to Marilyn Allen for all of your ongoing guidance, and the warmth that comes with it.

Thank you to design rockstars Carolyn Pulvino and Judy Alexander for creating such perfect (!) icons that give every single recipe page a special touch.

Thank you to Wes Crain, and the rest of my superfoods family at Navitas Naturals, for providing me with the honor of working with the best products in the world, while alongside the very best people.

Lastly, a big thanks to my neighbors and friends for all your juicy taste-testing, earnest feedback, and of course, laughs and love.

Best team ever.

QUICK REBOOT

DETOX & FLUSH

Acai Cherry Limeade	66	Fennel Herb	103	Parsnip Parsley	108
Acai Ginger	79	Fennel Mint	109	Pineapple Aronia Berry	86
Almond Celery	115	Fresh Vegetable Broth	156	Pineapple Cilantro	
Aronia Beet	150	Ginger Greens	99	Kombucha Spritzer	186
Bok Choy Mung Bean	113	Gingery Apple Broccoli	124	Pineapple Mangosteen	77
Burdock & Roots	127	Grapefruit Mint	98	Pomegranate Cucumber	69
Cantaloupe Ginger	62	Green Apple Kale	93	Purslane Celery	96
Cantaloupe Sea Buckthorn		Green Apple Kale Chia		Sea Buckthorn Beet	128
Granita	166	Fresca	178	Spectrum Juice	147
Carrot Dill	137	Green Fruit Pops	173	Spiced Pomegranate	81
Cashew Roots	144	Honeydew Mint Chia Fresca	181	Spicy Daikon	145
Celery Greens	101	Jicama Romaine	116	Spicy Greens	104
Chili Peach	74	Kumquat Cranberry	88	Spicy Papaya	70
Citrus Aloe	78	Lemon Chard	102	Spinach Hemp	122
Coconut Spirulina	123	Lime Greens	111	Spinach Pear	118
Cooling Kale	95	Maqui Grapefruit		Spirulina Watermelon	75
Cranberry-Orange Chia		Kombucha Spritzer	184	Sweet Spinach	106
Fresca	175	Master Cleanse Granita	164	Vanilla Greens	107
Cucumber Mint	114	Orange Mangosteen	63	Veggie Classic	119
Electrolyte Chia Lemonade	176	Parsnip Hemp	132	Watermelon Goji	65

SLIM & TONE

Aronia Beet	150	Cantaloupe Ginger	62	Cooling Kale	95
Fennel Aronia Berry	148	Cantaloupe Sea Buckthorn		Cranberry-Orange Chia	
Acai Berry Chia Fresca	179	Granita	166	Fresca	175
Acai Cherry Limeade	66	Carrot Cayenne	141	Cucumber Mint	114
Blood Orange & Sea		Celery Greens	101	Electrolyte Chia Lemonade	176
Buckthorn Mimosa	192	Cherry Merlot Granita	165	Fennel Herb	103
Blueberry Peach Agua Fresca	188	Chocolate Mint	121	Fennel Mint	109
Bok Choy Mung Bean	113	Citrus Aloe	78	Fresh Vegetable Broth	156
Burdock & Roots	127	Coconut Spirulina	123	Ginger Greens	99

Gingery Apple Broccoli	124	Lemon Chard	102	Spectrum Juice	147
Goji Mango Limeade	89	Lime Greens	111	Spiced Roots	157
Grapefruit Fennel	60	Mandarin Ginger		Spicy Daikon	145
Grapefruit Mint	98	Kombucha Spritzer	183	Spicy Greens	104
Green Apple Kale	93	Maqui Grapefruit		Spinach Pear	118
Green Apple Kale Chia Fresca	178	Kombucha Spritzer	184	Spirulina Watermelon	75
Green Fruit Pops	173	Master Cleanse Granita	164	Strawberry Lime Agua Fresca	189
Green Tea Goji Infusion	187	Pineapple Cilantro		Strawberry Wine Spritzer	191
Honeydew Mint Chia Fresca	181	Kombucha Spritzer	186	Vanilla Greens	107
Jicama Romaine	116	Purslane Celery	96	Veggie Classic	119
Kale Martini	196	Sea Buckthorn Bell Pepper	151	Watermelon Goji	65

STRENGTH & STAMINA

Acai Berry Chia Fresca	179	Electrolyte Chia Lemonade	176	Pineapple Mangosteen	77
Acai Cherry Limeade	66	Fresh Vegetable Broth	156	Plum Aronia Berry	80
Acai Ginger	79	Ginger Greens	99	Pomegranate Cucumber	69
Acai Grape	68	Goji Mango Limeade	89	Pomegranate-Acai Granita	170
Acai Yam	131	Green Apple Kale	93	Purslane Celery	96
Almond Celery	115	Green Apple Kale Chia Fresca	178	Raspberry Granita	168
Aronia Beet	150	Green Fruit Pops	173	Russian Sea Buckthorn	142
Berries & Cream	91	Green Tea Goji Infusion	187	Sea Buckthorn Beet	128
Burdock & Roots	127	Honeydew Mint Chia Fresca	181	Spectrum Juice	147
Cacao Pear	85	Kumquat Cranberry	88	Spiced Fresh Cider	153
Carrot Cayenne	141	Lavender Rose	159	Spiced Pomegranate	81
Carrot Dill	137	Lime Greens	111	Spiced Roots	157
Carrot Ginger Ice Cream	162	Lucuma Carrot	140	Spicy Greens	104
Carrot Goji	130	Maca Yam	136	Spicy Papaya	70
Carrot Maca	134	Maqui Grapefruit		Spinach Hemp	122
Cashew Roots	144	Kombucha Spritzer	184	Spirulina Watermelon	75
Celery Greens	101	Maqui Pear		Strawberry Kiwi	82
Chili Peach	74	Kombucha Sorbet	169	Strawberry Orange	59
Chocolate Mint	121	Orange Mangosteen	63	Strawberry Rhubarb	67
Chocolate-Mint Noni Soft		Parsnip Hemp	132	Sweet Potato Kale	112
Serve	161	Parsnip Parsley	108	Sweet Potato Protein	139
Citrus Apple	73	Pineapple Aronia Berry	86	Tomato Celery	149
Coconut Spirulina	123	Pineapple Cilantro		Volcano Hot Chocolate	154
Cranberry-Orange Chia Fresca	175	Kombucha Spritzer	186	Watermelon Goji	65

BEAUTY & ANTI-AGING

Acai Berry Chia Fresca	179	Fresh Vegetable Broth	156	Pineapple Aronia Berry	86
Acai Cherry Limeade	66	Ginger Greens	99	Pineapple Cilantro	
Acai Ginger	79	Grapefruit Fennel	60	Kombucha Spritzer	186
Acai Grape	68	Grapefruit Mint	98	Plum Aronia Berry	80
Acai Yam	131	Green Apple Kale	93	Pomegranate Cucumber	69
Almond Celery	115	Green Apple Kale Chia		Pomegranate-Acai Granita	170
Aronia Beet	150	Fresca	178	Purslane Celery	96
Berries & Cream	91	Green Fruit Pops	173	Raspberry Granita	168
Blood Orange & Sea		Green Tea Goji Infusion	187	Russian Sea Buckthorn	142
Buckthorn Mimosa	192	Honeydew Mint Chia		Sea Buckthorn Beet	128
Bok Choy Mung Bean	113	Fresca	181	Sea Buckthorn Bell Pepper	151
Cantaloupe Sea Buckthorn		Honeydew Wheatgrass		Spectrum Juice	147
Granita	166	Margarita	195	Spiced Pomegranate	81
Carrot Dill	137	Kale Martini	196	Spiced Roots	157
Carrot Ginger Ice Cream	162	Kumquat Cranberry	88	Spicy Daikon	145
Carrot Goji	130	Lavender Rose	159	Spicy Greens	104
Celery Greens	101	Lemon Chard	102	Spicy Papaya	70
Cherry Merlot Granita	165	Lime Greens	111	Spinach Hemp	122
Chili Peach	74	Lucuma Carrot	140	Spinach Pear	118
Chocolate Mint	121	Mandarin Ginger		Spirulina Watermelon	75
Chocolate-Mint Noni Soft		Kombucha Spritzer	183	Strawberry Kiwi	82
Serve	161	Mangosteen Peach		Strawberry Orange	59
Citrus Aloe	78	Sake Sangria	194	Strawberry Rhubarb	67
Citrus Apple	73	Maqui Grapefruit		Strawberry Wine Spritzer	191
Cooling Kale	95	Kombucha Spritzer	184	Sweet Potato Protein	139
Cranberry-Orange Chia Fresca	175	Maqui Pear		Sweet Spinach	106
Cucumber Mint	114	Kombucha Sorbet	169	Tomato Celery	149
Electrolyte Chia Lemonade	176	Master Cleanse Granita	164	Veggie Classic	119
Fennel Aronia Berry	148	Orange Mangosteen	63	Volcano Hot Chocolate	154
Fennel Mint	109	Parsnip Hemp	132	Watermelon Goji	65

ABOUT THE AUTHOR

Julie Morris is a Los Angeles-based natural food chef and advocate of whole, plant-based foods and superfoods. The bestselling author of *Superfood Smoothies* (Sterling 2013) and *Superfood Kitchen* (Sterling 2012), Julie has worked in the natural food industry for close to a decade as a recipe developer, writer, cooking show host, and spokesperson, and is the executive chef for Navitas Naturals, a fair trade company that specializes in 100% organic superfoods. Her mission is simple: to share recipes and nutrition tips that make a vibrantly healthy lifestyle both easy to achieve and delicious to follow. To learn more about Julie and superfoods visit juliemorris.net.

Photo: Oliver Barth

Photographer **Oliver Barth** was born and raised in Berlin, Germany. Barth is devoted to capturing the natural beauty of life in timeless images. He lives in Los Angeles, California. Visit Oliver Barth at ilovefoodphotography.com.

Photo: Steve Bonini